L. Boris

MINIMAL BRAIN DYSFUNCTION

Minimal Brain Dysfunction

by

MORTIMER D. GROSS, M.D.

Clinical Associate Professor of Psychiatry
University of Illinois
The Medical Center at Chicago

and

WILLIAM C. WILSON, M.D.

Clinical Assistant Professor of Neurology
University of Illinois
The Medical Center at Chicago

BRUNNER/MAZEL, *Publishers* ● NEW YORK

Preface

The data we are presenting in this volume are based on the neuropsychiatric, psychological and electroencephalographic examination of over 1000 children who were consecutive patients at the Fox Valley Mental Health Center in Elgin, Illinois. Although we have experience with another 1000 children seen in private practice over the past twelve years, we are confining our statistical treatment entirely to the mental health center children because they represent a precisely defined population from a large but limited geographical area for which we have a uniquely devised control series.

We acknowledge with gratitude the time and secretarial services provided by J. Aldene Ecker, director of the Fox Valley Mental Health Center. We are also grateful for the help in the statistical treatment and computer services provided by the CIBA Pharmaceutical Division.

MORTIMER D. GROSS, M.D.
WILLIAM C. WILSON, M.D.

Contents

Illustrations

Introduction

In recent years minimal brain dysfunction has come into prominence. There are both positive and negative aspects to this increased interest. On the one hand, it is one step further away from that period in child psychiatry when behavioral problems were automatically viewed as the direct result of adverse environmental influences and noxious parental handling. Evidence that there was organismic incapacity in the child to adapt positively to the circumstances of his life was frequently overlooked or reinterpreted in psychodynamic terms. On the other hand, "minimal cerebral dysfunction" is in danger of becoming an omnibus diagnosis. Such premature closure of diagnostic thought might well interfere with thorough investigation and eliminate the possibility of uncovering alternative or additional reasons for the youngster's behavioral difficulties. Even more ominous is the tendency to use such a diagnosis as an excuse for inaction. Such a nihilistic attitude can result in a failure to provide necessary therapeutic interventions or alterations in a stressful environment.

A well-defined study of minimal cerebral dysfunction is required at this particular time and this study by Gross and
Wilson appears to fill the need. It involves an examination of
1056 child patients at a mental health center, all of whom
received neurologic and electroencephalographic examinations in addition to the usual psychiatric and psychological
work-ups. The authors report a surprisingly high finding of
encephalographic abnormalities—approximately 50% of the
total sample. In an effort to control for bias, EEG's of school
children selected by teachers as being "normal" were mixed
with those of the clinical cases and subjected to a blind reading. The resultant 3.8% abnormal EEG's in the normal
population indicates that the very high figure obtained in
clinical cases alone does not stem from some peculiarity of the
criteria.

The authors speculate that there must have been a bias in
which certain children were retained by the schools for their
own services, with a skewed population being referred to the
mental health center. This report is not, therefore, to be considered a prevalence study in any sense. Rather, it is a detailed examination of children with behavior problems who
have some neurologic dysfunction as well. These children are
then compared with children with behavior disorder and no
neurologic dysfunction.

The orderly pursuit of appropriate questions is a prominent aspect of this volume. The authors make it clear that
they are fully aware of the diagnostic term "minimal brain
dysfunction" as it was defined by the task force of the National Institute of Neurological Diseases and Blindness in
1966. They also discuss the various euphemisms that have
since been employed for similar or partial behavioral patterns,
as well as the specificity of drug responsiveness of children
whose behaviors conform to the suggested descriptions. At all
times they maintain an open-minded approach to therapy.
For example, in examining the effects of medicative inter-

vention, the researchers routinely prescribed placebos as the first "medication." Parent and teacher guidance is automatically included in the treatment plan, and drug side effects are given careful consideration in the child's overall therapy program. In sum, the authors' open-minded approach to diagnosis and therapy makes this a thoroughly scientific enquiry possessing much needed information.

STELLA CHESS, M.D.
Professor of Child Psychiatry
New York University Medical Center

MINIMAL BRAIN
DYSFUNCTION

1

The Concept of Minimal
Brain Dysfunction

Until the early 1960's, the term "Minimal Brain Dysfunction" was hardly known to professionals in pediatrics, neurology, psychiatry, psychology or education, let alone the lay person. Now it has acquired a wide currency and is on the lips of teachers and parents everywhere in the United States. Even under other names—the terminology has ranged from "brain damage," "neurological handicap," "maturational lag," to the current official term, "Hyperkinetic Syndrome"—it had been a condition unknown to and undiagnosed by the great majority of clinicians who work with children.

Yet, one cannot believe that this condition arose *de novo* in one decade. The reason for this sudden appearance of a new syndrome can be understood by a brief excursion into the state of child psychiatry in the first half of this century. Psychoanalysis had created a true revolution in thought about child development, a field of study which prior to 1900 hardly existed at all in any form. So much new was learned about children through reconstruction of adults' memories of their own childhood as brought out in psychoanalytic therapy, and later through direct observation of children, that in a few decades the fields of child psychiatry and child psychology came to be dominated by psychoanalytic thinking, at least in the English-speaking world.

Like everything new, what was once revolutionary became, after a time, ultraconservative. A hard and fast doctrine soon permeated the thinking of clinicians: problems in children were due to traumatic or unhealthy experiences in early childhood; relationships with parents, especially the mother, were clearly the most influential on the child and hence were immediately indicted as the locus of the children's problems; psychotherapy for the parents (usually the mother) by a social worker, simultaneous with, but generally separate from, psychotherapy or play therapy for the child by a child psychiatrist or psychologist, became the standard treatment model. The success of this procedure in many cases led to the belief that *all* psychological problems of children—problems of behavior, neuroses, psychoses, learning disorders, speech disorders—had essentially the same etiology in disturbed family relationships and required the same treatment. Problems in learning were thus lumped together with other "emotional problems."

In the mid-1950's, the discovery of antipsychotic drugs and their tremendous impact on the treatment of mental disorders led to a resurgence of interest in the workings of the brain as the physical basis for the mind. Advances in cybernetics, computer models of the brain, electronmicroscopy of nervous tissue, and the chemistry of brain functioning led to increased interest in the relationship of problems of children (and adults) to an *internal* environment as well as external—that is, to the way their brains functioned or malfunctioned. This, of course, does not deny the importance of the external environment—parents, siblings, the neighborhood subculture, and the larger culture—but these are no longer seen as the *sole* factors in the etiology of psychological problems. For example, recent studies of adopted children comparing their psychological problems with those of their natural *and* adoptive parents have furnished conclusive evidence that genetic factors are extremely important and override environmental factors in a number of psychological disturbances (Rosenthal and Kety, 1968; Kety, 1971; Rosenthal, 1971).

The similarities between behavioral deviations exhibited by children with known brain malfunction (brain damage or dysplasia) and a large sub-group of children with problems of behavior or learning or both led to the concept of "minimal brain dysfunction." This concept assumes that these latter children have some dysfunction of their brain that is not severe enough to be manifested by the usual ("hard") neurological disturbances, such as motor weakness, spasticity, abnormalities in sensation, or pathologic reflexes, but is marked rather by minimal ("soft") neurologic disturbances, such as clumsiness, nystagmus, mixed or confused laterality.

Kanner (1949) was one of the first clinicians to attempt to separate certain disorders from the general field of psychological disturbances of children, and his description of autism is a well-known classic. Nevertheless, the perseverative assumption that *all* psychological disturbances must be based on disturbed parent-child relationships hindered an understanding of this syndrome; only recently has overwhelming evidence been presented that autism is a primitive way of coping with a disorganized brain (Rimland, 1964). Bender (1946, 1959, 1961) contributed enormously to the clarification of the relationship between brain and behavior of children. Most of her work, however, bears on children with disturbances so severe as to require hospitalization or institutionalization. The typical office or clinic patient still tended to be seen in terms of "emotional problems," meaning disturbed family relationships. The growth of family therapy and observations of the dynamic interplay of all family members when one was considered "sick"—the use of the term "identified patient" implying that all family members were "sick" but only the identified one was designated as such—led even further away from the notion that in some families a child may indeed have a true "sickness" in terms of brain dysfunction and that disturbed family relationships may *result* from this sickness rather than *cause* it.

Thomas, Chess, and Birch (1963, 1968) made a major contribution to understanding children through the concept of "temperament" as an inborn trait. They demonstrated how the temperament of a child affects relationships with other family members in an ongoing transaction. This is a far more sophisticated approach than the psychoanalytic concept of the "rejecting" or disturbed mother "causing" psychological impairment in children.

The first reports on the symptom of "hyperkinesis" in children appeared in the 1930's (Kramer and Pollnow, 1932; Kahn and Cohen, 1934). Soon after came reports of the usefulness of amphetamines in treating these children (Bradley, 1937). Interest in the electroencephalogram (EEG) and possible clinical-EEG correlates also developed at this time.

Ounsted (1955), in discussing epileptic children, listed the following signs manifested in the behavior of "brain injured children": (1) distractibility, (2) short attention span, (3) wide scatter on the test results when given formal intelligence tests, (4) fluctuation of mood with euphoria as the abiding background, (5) aggressive outbursts, (6) diminution or absence of spontaneously affectionate behavior, (7) lack of shyness, (8) lack of fear. In 1938, Jasper et al. published the first report demonstrating that in a group of disturbed, *non-epileptic* children a substantial portion had an abnormal EEG. Their patients came from a home for disturbed children. They wrote:

> It is concluded that abnormal brain function as revealed by the EEG is an important component in the aetio-

logical picture of the majority of a group of problem children whose disorder had been considered as primarily psychogenic previous to using this method of diagnosis.

It took two decades for this conception to infiltrate the body of clinical psychiatry. In 1962, Clements and Peters, reporting on brain dysfunctions of school age children, listed ten common characteristics: (1) hyperactivity, (2) specific learning defects in the presence of normal intelligence, (3) perceptual motor deficits, (4) impulsivity, (5) emotional instability, (6) short attention span, (7) coordination deficits, (8) distractibility, (9) equivocal neurologic signs, (10) frequent abnormal EEG. The similarities between this list and that of Ounsted for "brain injured children with epilepsy," that is, children with proven organic brain disease, are striking.

Pioneering in understanding the special educational needs of children with brain damage—with implication for the less severely impaired brain dysfunctional child—was the classic work of Strauss (1947, 1955). By creating an awareness of the need to differentiate various types of learning skills in individual children and to provide special educational techniques to teach children with brain impairment, he demonstrated that the diagnosis of brain impairment was not an academic exercise but had important educational consequences. The growing acceptance of the usefulness of medication for this condition further accentuated the importance of making a proper diagnosis.

In 1966, after three years of preparation, a task force sponsored by the National Institute of Neurological Diseases and Blindness published the first of a projected series on "Minimal Brain Dysfunction in Children." This monograph, published by the United States Department of Health, Education and Welfare, attempted to eliminate some of the confusion in terminology and conceptual frameworks (Clements, 1966).

Selected parts of this monograph are reproduced in Appendix A.

Since the publication of this report, the term "Minimal Brain Dysfunction" (MBD) has achieved wide currency, supplanting other descriptive terms except "Hyperkinetic Syndrome of Childhood," which is the official nomenclature in the *Diagnostic and Statistical Manual of Mental Disorders II* published by the American Psychiatric Association. The late 1960's have also seen a flood of reports on this condition so that whereas in the early part of that decade it was difficult to convince anyone that some problem children had a brain dysfunction, by 1970 many (though by no means all) pediatricians, child psychologists and psychiatrists had become quite familiar with the syndrome.

The major weakness of the definition of the United States Department of Health, Education and Welfare is the subjectivity in making the diagnosis. "Soft" neurological signs, by definition, are not neurologic signs for which there is a body of clinical-pathologic correlation as there is for the usual "hard" neurologic signs. An abnormal EEG may be considered objective evidence for brain dysfunction, but even here there is a difference among authorities as to what constitutes an abnormality, and some authorities assert that certain abnormalities are so common that they can have no clinical significance (Lombroso, 1966; Walter, 1960; Little, 1965). *The most compelling evidence for the existence of MBD as an entity is (1) the similarity as already noted between its symptoms and symptoms of children with proven organic brain disease; and (2) the remarkable response to certain medications, a response not found in non-MBD children.* This will be demonstrated in later chapters.

One of the major obstacles in arriving at a diagnosis of MBD is the fact that many of the symptoms are displayed only under stress or in groups with other children. Thus, in an office interview or in other one-to-one situations, *so many symptoms may be absent* that it does not seem possible that the child being observed is the same child being described by the parents and teachers. Failure to recognize this discrepancy has led to enormous confusion and even to skepticism that MBD actually exists (Gomez, 1967).

In this volume, we are attempting to analyze more precisely the nature of MBD and determine what laboratory and clinical correlations exist, as well as what treatments are effective.

2

Methodology of This Study

Patient Population

The Fox Valley Mental Health Center serves a population of 190,000 clustered in several suburban and semi-rural communities 35 miles west of Chicago. It is a low-cost, out-patient psychiatric clinic, fees being set on the basis of income, and it serves mostly Caucasian, middle-middle-class, lower-middle-class, and upper-lower-class families. Only one percent of our case load is black and one percent Latin-American. Half the children are referred by schools, one-fourth by the family, eight percent by physicians, and the remainder by clergy, courts, and other social agencies. Private psychiatric services in the community are scarce, so the Mental Health Center sees many families who might otherwise seek private care.

The school systems, with which the Center works closely, are considered quite above the national average in quality. Most of the schools have good social service coverage and undoubtedly many minor problems are handled by counselors, and thus are not referred to the Center.

The data presented in this volume represent findings on 1056 consecutive admissions of all children—defined as 18 years old or younger —who completed the diagnostic workup. The project was started in 1962 and completed in 1971, so that many of the patients have a follow up of over five years.

Origins of the Study

In the 1950's, one of us (WCW) had begun a project of routine EEG's for all admissions to one of the units at Elgin State Hospital. The high frequency of abnormalities found led to a curiosity about what routine EEG's would reveal on all out-patient admissions to a mental health center—patients who would have considerably milder psychiatric disturbances. To our surprise, abnormalities in out-patient children proved to be approximately 50%. The dramatic improvement with medication of one of a set of monozygotic twins (Case #583, Chapter 7) led us to re-examine our whole treatment philosophy. We found that in our case load were many children diagnosed then as "hypomanic" for whom the standard treatment program did not seem to work, despite an enormous input of time and energy. This standard program consisted of (1) intake interview by a social worker with parents; (2) interview of the child by a psychiatrist; (3) testing by a psychologist; (4) presentation of the case to the entire professional staff; (5) completion interview with the parents to discuss the staff's recommendations; and finally (6) a therapeutic program, usually protracted in time, with the child in play therapy and the parents seen collaboratively by a social worker. Needless to say, such a program soon saturated our professional time, as well as leaving us with many treatment failures.

With the instant success achieved in the twin in Case #583 (page 110), using about an hour of professional time, we searched the literature and found that others had indeed reported similar experiences. Presumably their experiences went unheeded because the idea of treating psychiatric problems in children with medications went so counter to the grain of traditional child psychiatry. With further experience we found so many children responding well to medication alone that we embarked on this research program, using the EEG as an additional diagnostic tool, and eventually obtaining our own electroencephalograph to minimize the cost. The number of children we were able to diagnose and treat increased tenfold.

A preliminary report was published in 1964 (Gross and Wilson); by 1971, we were able to accumulate the 1,000 cases we set for our goal.

Diagnostic Instruments Used

Each child was examined by a psychiatrist and given a psychiatric as well as a neurologic examination. Young children were generally examined in a playroom, older children in the office; at least one parent (or foster parent) was interviewed and a complete history obtained.

Each child was also given an EEG, with every effort being made to get a sleep record and a record with hyperventilation. The EEG was interpreted according to the method of Gibbs and Gibbs (1964). All the EEG's were read twice by the same electroencephalographer at an interval of several months to several years (only five of the re-readings produced a change in the final EEG impressions) .

About half the children had psychological testing. Most of the testing included a Wechsler Intelligence Scale for Children (WISC). Psychological testing was not done when the problems in school were minimal or when no other strong indications for such tests existed. All psychological tests were conducted by state-qualified psychologists.

For about a third of the children, parents were asked to fill out a questionnaire on behavior and neurotic traits, devised by Peterson and Quay (Peterson 1961). These were not a selected group of children, but rather children seen during the last third of our study when it became apparent that such a questionnaire would yield valuable data. The questionnaire (Figure 1) lists a number of traits and asks the responder to select one of three responses, "No;" "Yes, a little bit;" and "Yes, very much." The questionnaire was scored by assigning a value of zero to "No" responses; one to a response of "Yes, a little bit;" and two to responses of "Yes, very much;" the values were added for the total score. Although this method lumps together various symptoms, most of the latter refer to behavior disorders, and thus the total scores roughly relate to the severity of the behavior problems.

Control Series

Most control series of EEG's in "normal" children reveal an incidence of abnormalities around 10 to 15 percent, although there are wide variations. We thought it best to obtain our own control series, attempting to obtain as many "normal children" as we could find, since the defect of many control series is that they are based on non-patients—which is hardly the same as "normal," no matter how the latter may be defined.

Since most of the patients are referred by the school, and thus were selected by the teachers as "not normal," we thought it would be logical to ask teachers to select "normal" children from their classrooms. Through the cooperation of the school authorities this was done. The teachers were asked to select children" as we could find, since the defect of many control Parents were contacted and their cooperation was solicited. Children who had had seizures, serious head trauma, metabolic or glandular dysfunction were excluded. From the resulting list we selected 14 children from each grade level, half girls and half boys, for a total of 160 children. Each child had

OBSERVATIONS OF BEHAVIOR

Patient's Name _____   Date _____
                  Last   First   Middle Initial   Month   Day   Year

Observer(s)
Name(s) _____

Information Provided by: ☐ 1. MOTHER   ☐ 2. FATHER   ☐ 3. BOTH PARENTS   ☐ 4. OTHER RELATIVE
                    ☐ 5. FOSTER PARENTS   ☐ 6. OTHER - Specify _____

Test #1 2 3 4 5 *(circle one)*   Peterson - Quay Scale

PLEASE ANSWER ALL QUESTIONS	NO	YES - A LITTLE BIT	YES - VERY MUCH	REMARKS
Thumb sucking	☐	☐	☐	
Restlessness, inability to sit still	☐	☐	☐	
Attention-seeking, "show-off" behavior	☐	☐	☐	
Skin allergy	☐	☐	☐	
Doesn't know how to have fun; behaves like a little adult	☐	☐	☐	
Self-consciousness, easily embarrassed	☐	☐	☐	
Headaches	☐	☐	☐	
Disruptiveness; tendency to annoy and bother others	☐	☐	☐	
Feelings of inferiority	☐	☐	☐	
Dizziness, vertigo	☐	☐	☐	
Boisterousness, rowdiness	☐	☐	☐	
Crying over minor annoyances and hurts	☐	☐	☐	
Preoccupation; "in a world of his own"	☐	☐	☐	
Shyness, bashfulness	☐	☐	☐	
Social withdrawal, preference for solitary activities	☐	☐	☐	
Dislike for school	☐	☐	☐	
Jealousy over attention paid other children	☐	☐	☐	
Difficulty in bowel control, soiling	☐	☐	☐	
Prefers to play with younger children	☐	☐	☐	
Short attention span	☐	☐	☐	
Lack of self-confidence	☐	☐	☐	
Inattentiveness to what others say	☐	☐	☐	
Easily flustered and confused	☐	☐	☐	
Lack of interest in environment, generally "bored" attitude	☐	☐	☐	
Fighting	☐	☐	☐	
Nausea, vomiting	☐	☐	☐	
Temper tantrums	☐	☐	☐	
Reticence, secretiveness	☐	☐	☐	
Truancy from school	☐	☐	☐	
Hypersensitivity; feelings easily hurt	☐	☐	☐	
Laziness in school and in performance of other tasks	☐	☐	☐	
Anxiety, chronic general fearfulness	☐	☐	☐	
Irresponsibility, undependability	☐	☐	☐	
Excessive daydreaming	☐	☐	☐	
Masturbation	☐	☐	☐	
Hay fever and/or asthma	☐	☐	☐	
Tension, inability to relax	☐	☐	☐	
Disobedience, difficulty in disciplinary control	☐	☐	☐	
Depression, chronic sadness	☐	☐	☐	
Unco-operativeness in group situations	☐	☐	☐	

RCI 10B (PAGE 1 OF 3) 966

Figure 1.
Peterson-Quay Questionnaire (p. 1.)

	NO	YES - A LITTLE BIT	YES - VERY MUCH	REMARKS
Aloofness, social reserve	☐	☐	☐	
Passivity, suggestibility; easily led by others	☐	☐	☐	
Clumsiness, awkwardness, poor muscular co-ordination	☐	☐	☐	
Stuttering	☐	☐	☐	
Hyperactivity; "always on the go"	☐	☐	☐	
Distractibility	☐	☐	☐	
Destructiveness in regard to his own and/others' property	☐	☐	☐	
Negativism, tendency to do the opposite of what is required	☐	☐	☐	
Impertinence, sauciness	☐	☐	☐	
Sluggishness, lethargy	☐	☐	☐	
Drowsiness	☐	☐	☐	
Profane language, swearing, cursing	☐	☐	☐	
Prefers to play with older children	☐	☐	☐	
Nervousness, jitteriness, jumpiness; easily startled	☐	☐	☐	
Irritability; hot-tempered, easily aroused to anger	☐	☐	☐	
Enuresis, bed-wetting	☐	☐	☐	
Stomach aches, abdominal pain	☐	☐	☐	
Specific fears, e.g., of dogs, of the dark	☐	☐	☐	

TOTAL SCORE

PERSONALITY PROBLEM SCORE _____

CONDUCT DISORDER SCORE _____

	NO	YES - A LITTLE BIT	YES - VERY MUCH	
Seizures	☐	☐	☐	
Bizarre content of thought	☐	☐	☐	
Fluctuating performance	☐	☐	☐	
Socially inept behavior	☐	☐	☐	
Tics	☐	☐	☐	
Danger to self	☐	☐	☐	
Danger to others	☐	☐	☐	
Excessive talking	☐	☐	☐	

Werry - Weiss - Peters Activity Scale

DURING MEALS

	NO	YES - A LITTLE BIT	YES - VERY MUCH	
Up and Down at table	☐	☐	☐	
Interrupts without regard	☐	☐	☐	
Wriggling	☐	☐	☐	
Fiddles with things	☐	☐	☐	
Talks excessively	☐	☐	☐	

TELEVISION

	NO	YES - A LITTLE BIT	YES - VERY MUCH	
Gets up and down during program	☐	☐	☐	
Wriggles	☐	☐	☐	
Manipulates objects or body	☐	☐	☐	
Talks incessantly	☐	☐	☐	
Interrupts	☐	☐	☐	

DOING HOME-WORK

	NO	YES - A LITTLE BIT	YES - VERY MUCH	
Gets up and down	☐	☐	☐	
Wriggles	☐	☐	☐	
Manipulates objects or body	☐	☐	☐	
Talks incessantly	☐	☐	☐	
Requires adult supervision or attendance	☐	☐	☐	

RCI 108 (PAGE 2 OF 3) 968

Figure 1
Peterson-Quay Questionnaire (p. 2)

	NO	YES - A LITTLE BIT	YES - VERY MUCH
PLAY			
Inability for quiet play	☐	☐	☐
Constantly changing activity	☐	☐	☐
Seeks parental attention	☐	☐	☐
Talks excessively	☐	☐	☐
Disrupts other's play	☐	☐	☐
SLEEP			
Difficulty settling down for sleep	☐	☐	☐
Inadequate amount of sleep	☐	☐	☐
Restless during sleep	☐	☐	☐
BEHAVIOR AWAY FROM HOME (except School)			
Restlessness during travel	☐	☐	☐
Restlessness during shopping (includes touching everything)	☐	☐	☐
Restlessness during church/movies	☐	☐	☐
Restlessness during visiting friends, relatives, etc.	☐	☐	☐
SCHOOL BEHAVIOR			
Up and down	☐	☐	☐
Fidgets, wriggles, touches	☐	☐	☐
Interrupts teacher or other children excessively	☐	☐	☐
Constantly seeks teacher's attention	☐	☐	☐
TOTAL SCORE			

Figure 1
Peterson-Quay Questionnaire (p. 3)

an EEG with sleep record and hyperventilation. Parents were asked to fill out a Peterson-Quay questionnaire which was scored the same way as the patients' questionnaires were scored. The EEG's were mixed in with routine EEG's so that the electroencephalographer would have no way of identifying them as controls.

The Basic Data Collected

The following data were available on each child:

1. Age
2. Sex
3. Presence of mental retardation and degree of retardation scaled from 0 to 6 according to severity using the

classification of Diagnostic and Statistical Manual of
Mental Disorders—II.

    0. Not retarded
    1. Questionable; on WISC marked discrepancy
       between Verbal and Performance IQ, one
       being greater than 85 and the other less than
       78
    2. Upper borderline IQ 78 to 85
    3. Lower borderline IQ 68 to 77
    4. Mild retardation, IQ 52 to 67
    5. Moderate retardation, IQ 36 to 51
    6. Severe retardation, IQ 20 to 35

4. Degree of psychiatric impairment on a scale of 0 to 6.
This was the clinical judgment of the psychiatrist
who examined the patient's record. Disorders of behavior, mood, thought and learning were evaluated,
but mental retardation was not considered psychiatric
impairment unless there was, in addition, either behavior, mood, or thought disorder, or unless learning
was impaired beyond what would be expected con-
sidering his IQ.

The definitions of the numerical ratings are as follows.

    0. Indicates no psychiatric impairment of any
       significance. Usually this is found in children
       who are referred for psychological testing for
       evaluation of possible mental retardation. Oc-
       casionally, it will be found in a case referred
       to us as a disturbed child, but actually a
       normal child reacting to a disturbed environ-
       ment.
    1. Refers to patients with such mild psychiatric
       impairment that some observers (family and/
       or teachers) would see a problem, while
       others would see no problem.
    2. Refers to cases where significant psychiatric
       impairment is demonstrated but that is not
       incapacitating at all, although some definite
       disability is observable.

3. Refers to average psychiatric impairment; a fair degree of disability handicapping the child in his activities in a clear, perceptible way. Such a child would be considered by observers to have an impairment but would not be considered, for example, as the worst child in the class or the worst child in the block. This degree of impairment would be tolerable if necessary by both family and school.

4. Refers to more severe impairment which is not tolerable by home or school. There would be considerable pressure on or by the family to do something about such a child.

5. Refers to a child who is barely supportable in the community. Such a child might be recommended for removal from the community, but nevertheless be able to squeeze by. However, he is pinpointed by all concerned as a severe problem.

6. Refers to a child who is insupportable in the community, and whose impairment is so great that hospitalization or institutionalization is necessary.

5. EEG Type

  0. Normal, awake and asleep
  1. 6 Hz* or 14/6 Hz positive spikes
  2. 6 Hz positive spike-waves
  3. Fast waves
  4. Negative and diphasic spikes
  5. Negative spike-waves
  6. Slow waves
  7. Notched waves
  8. Hyperventilation abnormalities
  9. Slow waves plus other abnormalities
10. Normal awake only—no sleep record obtained.

* A Hertz (Hz) is one cycle per second.

For statistical purposes, the various types were collected into four groups according to estimated degree of abnormality of the EEG:

I. Types 0 and 10 (normal)

II. Types 1, 2 and 3 (positive spikes, positive spike-waves, and fast waves)

III. Types 4 and 5 (negative and diphasic spikes and spike-waves)

IV. Types 6, 7, 8, 9 (slow waves with or without other abnormalities)

6. History of Seizures

0. Never had any seizures
1. Occasional febrile seizures as an infant
2. Occasional non-febrile seizures, less than one a year
3. Periodic seizures; definite presence of epilepsy

7. Clinical Impression of Brain Dysfunction

0. No clinical evidence of any brain dysfunction
1. Definite evidence of MBD (using criteria on page 19)
2. Definite evidence of MBD plus some evidence of brain damage (perseveration, aphasia, bizarreness, severe speech defect)

8. Presence of "hard" neurologic signs

0 Absence
1. Presence

The following data were available on some but not all of the patients:

9. Peterson-Quay Questionnaire Score
10. IQ Score—either WISC Full Scale or other IQ tests
11. Verbal IQ on WISC
12. Performance IQ on WISC

13. Difference between Verbal and Performance IQ on WISC (V -P)

14. Response to placebo (scored as follows) :

     —2. Considerably worse

     —1. Slightly worse—indicating a definite impression that the patient was worse during the period of time he was using the medication and seemed to improve when medication was discontinued.

     0. No significant change

     1. Slight improvement but of such degree as to leave some doubt as to whether the improvement was real or imagined.

     2. Mild improvement with some objective evidence, such as teacher's reports, improved grades, better report cards.

     3. Moderate improvement—still not what one would expect from a normal child, but the improvement would be unequivocal and demonstrated by concrete observations (such as improved grades) from teachers, parents, and other observers.

     4. Marked improvement—indicating a very good improvement in which all observers agreed that there had been a major change in the patient for the better in that many of the symptoms have disappeared or improved to such an extent that the child was a minor problem now as compared to a major problem before.

     5. Almost total relief from symptoms, either with no residual symptoms or residual symptoms of a relatively insignificant nature.

15. Response to exploratory medication, that is, medications initially prescribed to determine which worked best on a preliminary trial (scored the same as Item 14).

16. Response to definitive medication, indicating medication had been tried at an optimum dosage level for at least a half year (scored the same as Item 14).

17. Duration of treatment in years. This includes only those treated a half year or more.
18. Adverse reactions or side effects from medication:

    0. No adverse reaction; no side effects, or only trivial, transient side effects.

    1. Mild side effects not of a degree to warrant discontinuing medication.

    2. Significant side effects but not of degree to warrant discontinuing medication if patient is sufficiently benefited.

    3. Severe side effects which warrant immediately discontinuing medication.

All data were processed through a computer to obtain maximum information about intercorrelations of all variables.

The Criteria Used for the Diagnosis of Minimal Brain Dysfunction

Four major factors used for diagnosis were history, EEG, psychological tests, and neuropsychiatric examination.

1. The history of an MBD child is frequently so "classical" that it is difficult to arrive at any other diagnosis unless it be brain damage. The following traits were considered typical of MBD, and if about half were present, a diagnosis of MBD was considered very likely.

a. Hyperactivity—on the go all the time
b. Short attention span for age
c. Distractibility
d. Overreaction to emotional stimuli
e. Impulsiveness
f. Inconsistency and unpredictability
g. Difficulty "getting through" or "reaching"
h. Muscular incoordination
i. Speech defects
j. Lack of appropriate fear
k. Lack of learning from experience
l. Lack of response to punishment

    m. Perceptual deficits
    n. Temper tantrums

2. EEG—an abnormality in EEG was almost always accepted as evidence for MBD.* A few exceptions were made when there were no supporting data from other sources.

3. Psychological testing frequently, but not always, showed distortions in the Bender-Gestalt test, unevenness in performance and scattering of sub-test scores on the WISC, as well as perceptual deficits and specific learning disabilities. Projective tests often showed impulsivity and explosiveness.**

4. The neuropsychiatric examination frequently, but not always, revealed fidgetiness, short attention span, muscular clumsiness, a tendency to rush through tasks, immaturity, lack of appropriate shyness or cautiousness.

Clinical Procedures

Each request for service for a given patient is first discussed at an Intake Staff meeting. Before the first interview with a psychiatrist, an EEG will have been ordered and done, and if psychological tests are thought necessary, they will be requested and will usually be available also. Occasionally other laboratory tests, such as tests for thyroid function or a brain scan, will be ordered. At the initial interview with the psychiatrist, an effort is made to reach a specific diagnosis. Usually, because the psychological and laboratory data are al-

---

* It is known that abnormal fast waves may appear on the EEG if the patient is taking certain medications, especially tranquilizers; in only one case was any medication used at the time the EEG was taken (other than chloral hydrate, which was used to induce sleep, and which is known to have no effect on the EEG).

** It should be emphasized that until recently psychologists considered as signs of "organicity" certain types of dysfunctions such as marked difficulty copying the block designs used on the various Wechsler tests. These signs of organicity correlate with gross deterioration of intellectual functioning, such as found in senility. They cannot be expected to correlate with the much more subtle evidence of brain dysfunction found in the typical MBD patients. Thus, when psychologists report "no evidence of organicity," they are by no means excluding minimal brain dysfunction.

ready available, this is possible. If a definite diagnosis of MBD is made, based on the overall consideration of history, EEG, psychological tests and neuropsychiatric examination, the nature of the diagnosis is explained to the parents, care being taken to avoid the term "brain damage," which has alarming connotations to lay persons. They are also given some instructions about coping with the problems, and then medication is dispensed or prescribed. Except for 50 cases in which placebos were prescribed in a "double blind technique," all cases involved the use of placebo "single blind," that is, the raters (parents and teachers) were unaware that one of the medications was inert, but the investigators were aware of this.

Usually placebos were prescribed the first week or two and then active medication, chosen at an average dose, for the next one or two weeks. For most cases, a third and fourth medication were also prescribed in order to explore the comparative effect of each. The usual treatment schedule followed this order:

1. Placebo—one or two weeks using tablets identical to methylphenidate in appearance.
2. D-amphetamine—one to two weeks; usual dose 1¼ mg, morning and noon, up to age 4; 2½ mg, morning and noon, ages 5 to 7; 5 mg, morning and 2½ mg, noon, ages 8 to 9; 5 mg, morning and noon or 10 mg time capsule, ages 10 and up.
3. Methylphenidate (Ritalin)—one to two weeks; usual dose 2½ mg, morning and noon, up to age 4; 5 mg, morning and noon, ages 5 to 7; 10 mg, morning and 5 mg noon, ages 8 and 9; 10 mg, morning and noon, age 10 and up.
4. Imipramine or desipramine—one to two weeks; usual dose 10 mg at bedtime until age 5; 20 mg at bedtime, ages 6 and 7; 25 mg at bedtime, age 8 to 12; 50 mg at bedtime, age 13 and up.

The placebo was given first since it would be expected that the role of suggestion or any improvement in management would be greater immediately following the interview than at a later time. The parents were asked to keep written records of the child's behavior and the teachers were asked to do the same. No time was allowed for one medication to wash out before starting another, since it was quickly apparent that changes in response to medication were present the very first day it was tried. Imipramine and desipramine were used last because of their longer duration of action. The two were used interchangeably depending on their availability (no difference was ever observed between the medications). For this reason, we will hereafter refer to these two medications collectively as des/imipramine. No children were refused medication in order to constitute a control group, as the need for treatment was so great that it did not appear ethical to withhold treatment. A comparison group was drawn, however, from children seen before we had begun to treat MBD with medication, and from cases where parents refused treatment.

3

Syndrome Derived from
Statistical Data

In this chapter we will summarize the data we have accumulated and the statistical treatment of the data in order to refine and define the syndrome of MBD, distinguish it from non-MBD and controls, and describe the intercorrelations which may be expected.

Of the 1056 patients, the clinical diagnosis of MBD was made for 817, or 77.4%.

Age

Our patients ranged in age from 2 to 18. The distribution is shown in Table 1. The mean age is 9.3, the median is 9, the mode, 8; the standard deviation, 3.5. The age distribution for girls is somewhat different than for boys, with larger numbers in the extremes of age, as shown in Table 2. Nevertheless, there is no statistically significant difference between ages of boys as opposed to girls ($t=0.78$, $p >0.2$). When age distribution is separated into MBD and non-MBD children, as shown in Table 3, it is clear that the diagnosis of brain dys-

TABLE 1

Distribution of Cases by Age

Age	Number	Percent
2	6	0.6
3	23	2.2
4	37	3.5
5	56	5.3
6	104	9.8
7	133	12.6
8	152	14.4
9	101	9.6
10	97	9.2
11	73	6.9
12	58	5.5
13	63	6.0
14	56	5.3
15	35	3.3
16	34	3.2
17	18	1.7
18	10	0.9
	1056	100.0

TABLE 2

Distribution of Age by Sex

Age	Number of Boys	Number of Girls
2 to 6	162 (20.6%)	64 (23.6%)
7 to 13	520 (66.2%)	157 (57.9%)
14 to 18	103 (13.1%)	50 (18.5%)
Total	785 (99.9%)	271 (100.0%)

TABLE 3

Distribution of Age by Presence or Absence of MBD

Age	Number of MBD Patients	Number of Non-MBD Patients	Total
2 to 6	201 (89.0%)	25 (11.0%)	226 (100%)
7 to 13	543 (80.2%)	134 (19.8%)	677 (100%)
14 to 18	73 (47.7%)	80 (52.3%)	153 (100%)
Total	817 (77.4%)	239 (22.6%)	1056 (100%)

function tends to be correlated inversely with age ($r=-0.32$, $p < 0.001$). What this means, we believe, is that young children who are disturbed enough to be brought to a physician are somewhat more likely to have MBD, while the older child, especially the adolescent, is more likely to have "emotional," non-MBD problems.

Three other variables correlated significantly with age: degree of psychiatric impairment; degree of retardation; severity of EEG. These will be discussed under the appropriate headings later in the chapter.

Sex

Of 1056 patients, 785 or 74.3% were boys, a ratio of male to female of 2.9. If one limits the data to MBD children, 639 or 78.2% were boys; 178 or 21.8% were girls, a male-female ratio of 3.6. This ratio of boys to girls is similar to findings of other researchers.

For boys, the percentage who have MBD is greater than for girls and the degree of psychiatric impairment is somewhat greater for boys than for girls. These data are outlined in Tables 4 and 5. For both these characteristics, the differences are statistically significant ($p<0.001$).

There was no important relationship between sex and the following variables: severity of EEG, IQ, history of seizures.

Chief Complaints

An analysis was made of the chief complaints (made by the parent or parents) at the time of the initial interview. The first three complaints mentioned were taken as the chief complaints. In some cases only one or two complaints were mentioned, so the data averaged less than three complaints per patient (actually 2.4 complaints per patient for both MBD and non-MBD categories). The data were divided into MBD

TABLE 4

Presence of MBD vs. Sex

	Boys		Girls	
Non-MBD	146	(18.6%)	93	(34.3%)
MBD	639	(81.4%)	178	(65.7%)
Total	785	(100.0%)	271	(100.0%)

($\chi^2=27.5$, $p<0.001$)

TABLE 5

Degree of Psychiatric Impairment vs. Sex

Degree of Psychiatric Impairment	Boys		Girls	
0	18	(2.3%)	17	(6.3%)
1	43 }	(31.5%)	32 }	(41.7%)
2	204 }		81 }	
3	278 }	(53.5%)	81 }	(40.2%)
4	142 }		28 }	
5	76 }	(12.7%)	23 }	(11.8%)
6	24 }		9 }	
	785	(100.0%)	271	(100.0%)

(t=3.76, p<0.001)

patients and non-MBD patients for comparison and are detailed in Table 6.

The major differences that emerge between MBD and non-MBD patients can be summarized as follows. In MBD patients, the complaints cluster around five major factors: (1) underachievement, learning problems; (2) restlessness; (3) temper outbursts; (4) aggressiveness; (5) distractibility, poor concentration. These five factors account for 64% of the total complaints. It should be noted that the following additional symptoms are significantly more common for MBD than for non-MBD children: poor muscular coordination, enuresis and encopresis, and fighting. It should also be noted

TABLE 6

Chief Complaints for MBD and Non-MBD Patients

Presenting Complaint	Percent of Patients Having This Complaint	
	MBD	Non-MBD
Underachievement, learning problems	75.4	38.5
Restlessness, hyperactivity	24.9	7.7
Temper outbursts	19.2	13.8
Aggressiveness, hostility	18.9	30.0
Distractible, poor concentration	17.0	4.6
Insecure, anxious, poor self-concept	12.1	23.8
Depression, moody, cries frequently	9.7	25.4
Poor muscular coordination	9.2	3.8
Enuresis, encopresis	8.9	3.1
Fighting	7.3	2.3
Rebelliousness	6.8	21.5
"Can't get through" to him	6.2*	5.3*
Headaches, stomachaches, insomnia	4.3	13.3
Stealing	4.3	6.9
Daydreams excessively	4.0*	3.8*
Lying	3.8*	4.6*
Running away, truancy	3.5	13.1
Sexual acting-out	2.4	6.9
Destructive	1.9	4.6
Attempted or threatened suicide	1.6*	2.3*
Autism	0.8*	0.8*
Jealousy	0.8	4.6
School phobia	0.5	2.3

* Difference not statistically significant

that underachievement in school is complained of more frequently than restlessness.

For non-MBD patients, the major clustering is as follows: (1) underachievement, learning problems; (2) aggressiveness, hostility; (3) depression, moodiness, frequent crying; (4) insecurity, anxiety, poor self-concept; (5) rebelliousness; (6) temper outbursts; (7) headaches, stomachaches, insomnia; (8) running away, truancy.

These eight factors account for 74% of the total chief complaints. It should be noted that there are three factors which are highly loaded in both MBD and non-MBD patients: (1)

underachievement; (2) aggressiveness; (3) temper outbursts. Restlessness and distractibility are overwhelmingly represented in MBD patients, while depression, insecurity, psychosomatic complaints, rebelliousness and running away are much more strongly represented in non-MBD patients. In addition to the aforementioned symptoms, the following symptoms are significantly more common for non-MBD than for MBD patients: school phobias, jealousy, destructiveness, and sexual acting out.

It would thus appear that the factors of restlessness and distractibility are highly important in distinguishing the MBD from the non-MBD patients. Since these factors went into the original formulation of the concept of MBD, this is hardly surprising; nevertheless, it does confirm statistically what has been assumed impressionistically. These, plus the other factors related to MBD, all point in the direction of defects in control systems, including muscle control, emotional control, bowel and bladder control, as well as systems involved in learning. It is interesting that the factor "fighting" is more heavily loaded for MBD patients, whereas "aggressiveness, hostility, and rebelliousness" are more heavily loaded for non-MBD patients. Fighting is more explosive and non-directional, whereas rebelliousness and hostility are more related to specific persons, and this goes along with the concept of defects in control systems.

Factors Elicited by the Peterson-Quay Questionnaire

This questionnaire was specifically designed to elicit supposed MBD symptoms; it does not begin to cover the spectrum of psychiatric disturbance and ignores many types of symptoms. Nevertheless, this questionnaire, filled out by one or both parents, yields important data. Table 7 lists the average response for MBD and non-MBD patients and for controls. The responses are an indication of frequency of

TABLE 7

Results of Peterson-Quay Questionnaire for MBD and
Non-MBD Patients and Controls

Questions Responded to	Average Weighted Score		
	MBD Patients	Control	Non-MBD Patients
1. Restlessness, inability to sit still	1.63	0.37	1.07
2. Hyperactivity, "always on the go"	1.51	0.37	0.67
3. Distractibility	1.49	0.21	0.78
4. Short attention span	1.35	0.14	0.74
5. Inattentiveness to what others say	1.35	0.25	0.90
6. Excessive talking	1.33	0.31	0.60
7. Disobedience; difficulty in disciplinary control	1.33	0.12	1.00
8. Hypersensitivity, feelings easily hurt	1.29	0.45	1.00
9. Disruptiveness; tendency to annoy or bother others	1.29	0.25	0.95
10. Crying over minor annoyances or hurts	1.29	0.37	0.69
11. Attention seeking, "show-off" behavior	1.27	0.41	0.81
12. Fighting	1.22	0.41	0.69
13. Irritability; hot-tempered, easily aroused to anger	1.20	0.27	0.98
14. Negativism, tendency to do the opposite of what is required	1.18	0.04	0.62
15. Boisterousness, rowdiness	1.16	0.25	0.71
16. Irresponsibility, undependability	1.14	0.08	0.74
17. Tension, inability to relax	1.14	0.20	0.74
18. Nervousness, jitteriness, jumpiness, easily startled	1.14	0.17	0.93
19. Lack of self-confidence	1.12	0.24	1.02
20. Laziness in school and in performance of other tasks	1.06	0.13	0.97
21. Uncooperativeness in group situations	1.02	0.04	0.55
22. Impertinence, sauciness	0.98	0.35	0.57
23. Feelings of inferiority	0.96	0.23	0.76
24. Easily flustered and confused	0.94	0.14	0.76
25. Destructiveness in regard to his own and/or others' property	0.94	0.04	0.45
26. Temper tantrums	0.92	0.16	0.52
27. Jealousy over attention paid other children	0.90	0.25	0.88
28. Lack of interest in environment, generally "bored" attitude	0.85	0.08	0.76
29. Fluctuating performance	0.80	0.08	0.43
30. Self-consciousness, easily embarrassed	0.78	0.58	1.00
31. Dislike for school	0.69	0.03	0.67
32. Socially inept behavior	0.67	0.03	0.19
33. Preoccupation; "in a world of his own"	0.67	0.23	0.64

Questions Responded to	*Average Weighted Score*		
	MBD Patients	*Control*	*Non-MBD Patients*
34. Anxiety; chronic general fearfulness	0.59	0.08	0.60
35. Passivity; suggestibility; easily led by others	0.59	0.23	0.79
36. Prefers to play with younger children	0.57	0.04	0.36
37. Excessive daydreaming	0.55	0.03	0.55
38. Clumsiness, awkwardness, poor muscular coordination	0.53	0.10	0.31
39. Reticence, secretiveness	0.53	0.09	0.67
40. Enuresis, bedwetting	0.45	0.11	0.38
41. Prefers to play with older children	0.43	0.35	0.38
42. Depression, chronic sadness	0.43	0.01	0.43
43. Shyness, bashfulness	0.43	0.39	0.62
44. Thumbsucking	0.43	0.09	0.14
45. Specific fears, e.g., of dark, of dogs	0.39	0.23	0.33
46. Bizarre content of thought	0.37	0.04	0.17
47. Headaches	0.37	0.14	0.33
48. Profane language, cursing, swearing	0.34	0.03	0.38
49. Stomachaches, abdominal pain	0.33	0.10	0.38
50. Aloofness, social reserve	0.31	0.08	0.45
51. Social withdrawal, preference for solitary activity	0.31	0.07	0.50
52. Sluggishness, lethargy	0.27	0.01	0.45
53. Danger to others	0.27	0.01	0.14
54. Doesn't know how to have fun, behaves like a little adult	0.20	0.05	0.48
55. Skin allergy	0.20	0.10	0.10
56. Drowsiness	0.20	0.00	0.19
57. Hay fever, asthma	0.18	0.11	0.14
58. Difficulty in bowel control, soiling	0.14	0.01	0.07
59. Nausea, vomiting	0.12	0.03	0.10
60. Truancy from school	0.10	0.02	0.10
61. Dizziness, vertigo	0.08	0.01	0.10
62. Danger to self	0.08	0.01	0.19
63. Tics	0.04	0.02	0.10
64. Stuttering	0.02	0.01	0.02
65. Seizures	0.00	0.00	0.05

symptoms with some weighting for severity (a response "yes, very much," is graded twice as much as response "yes, a little bit").

First observations show a tremendous contrast between patients and controls. In the questionnaire, some items were included as "fillers," for example, "skin allergy"; and these fillers show no significant difference between patients and controls. Aside from the fillers, only the items "self-consciousness, easily embarrassed," "shyness, bashfulness," have an incidence in normal controls approaching that of patients.

The major items which showed clear-cut greater incidence in MBD over non-MBD patients are listed below in order of decreasing ratios of MBD to non-MBD patients.

1. Socially inept behavior
2. Hyperactivity
3. Excessive talking
4. Destructiveness in regard to own and/or other's property
5. Distractibility
6. Negativeness
7. Crying over minor annoyances or hurts
8. Fluctuating performance
9. Uncooperativeness in group situations
10. Short attention span
11. Fighting
12. Temper tantrums
13. Impertinence, sauciness
14. Clumsiness, awkwardness, poor muscular coordination
15. Boisterousness, rowdiness
16. Attention-seeking, "show-off" behavior
17. Tension, inability to relax
18. Irresponsibility, undependability
19. Restlessness, inability to sit still
20. Inattentiveness to what others say

These symptoms, in general, match the MBD symptoms listed in the section on Chief Complaints, but there are quantitative differences. The questionnaire did not deal with learning problems, so that the major complaint, underachievement, is not present at all.

The following items showed greater incidence for non-

MBD over MBD patients. They are listed in order of decreasing ratios.

1. Doesn't know how to have fun, behaves like a little adult
2. Sluggishness, lethargy
3. Social withdrawal, preference for solitary activity
4. Shyness, bashfulness
5. Aloofness, social reserve
6. Passivity, suggestibility; easily led by others
7. Self-consciousness, easily embarrassed
8. Reticence, secretiveness

Unexplained is the low incidence of depression; in contrast to the data for Chief Complaints, depression was rated equally for MBD and non-MBD patients. It may be that "depression" is not as well understood by parents as "moodiness and frequent crying," which was found much more frequently in the chief complaints for non-MBD children.

Thus, for MBD children, we see a pattern of (1) dyscontrol of many systems; (2) defects in attention; (3) social ineptness; (4) fluctuations in performance. In line with this latter factor is the observation that parents frequently refer to their children as a "Dr. Jekyll and Mr. Hyde." It should also be noted that enuresis was reported considerably more often in MBD than non-MBD children, and both considerably more often than for the control series.

The overall Peterson-Quay score ranged from 5 to 141, with a mean of 66 and a standard deviation of 28. The sample size was 398. Distribution of Peterson-Quay scores is shown in Table 8.

For MBD children, the average score was 68, considerably higher than for non-MBD children, for which it was 49.

The relationship between Peterson-Quay score versus brain dysfunction is highly significant ($\chi^2=19$; $p<0.001$). There is also a positive correlation between Peterson-Quay score and

Table 8

Distribution of Peterson-Quay Questionnaire Scores

Score	Number of Cases	Percent
5 to 20	18	4.5
21 to 38	51	12.8
39 to 55	82	20.6
56 to 72	87	21.9
73 to 89	68	17.0
90 to 106	56	14.0
107 to 123	23	5.8
124 to 141	13	3.3

Table 9

Distribution of Degree of Psychiatric Impairment

Psychiatric Impairment	Number of Patients	Percent
0	35	3.1
1	75	7.1
2	285	27.0
3	359	34.0
4	170	16.1
5	99	9.4
6	33	3.1

the degree of psychiatric impairment, which is what would be expected if the Peterson-Quay score is meaningful ($r=0.35$; $p<0.001$). The Peterson-Quay score had no other significant correlations.

Psychiatric Impairment

This measurement is a quantified estimate of impairment in behavior, thought, mood, learning processes, but excludes mental retardation as an impairment; that is, children who were retarded were judged for the presence of psychiatric symptoms in the same way as non-retarded children. The impairment was rated 0 to 6 as described in the previous chapter.

TABLE 10

Psychiatric Impairment vs. Age

| Psychiatric Impairment | Number of Cases | | | |
	Age 2 to 5	Age 6 to 13	Age 15 to 18	Total
0	14	16	5	35
1	7	61	7	75
2	25	241	19	285
3	41	271	47	359
4	18	118	34	170
5	12	57	30	99
6	5	17	11	33
Total	122	781	153	1056

(r=0.21, p<0.001)

For the 1056 patients, the distribution of degree of psychiatric impairment is shown in Table 9. The average is 2.93, which is close to the number 3 arbitrarily assigned to "average impairment" in constructing the quantified grades of impairment. As already mentioned, psychiatric impairment relates somewhat with sex (Table 5), girls showing less impairment. There is also a positive correlation with age, shown in Table 10. This correlation appears to reflect the increased seriousness of psychiatric disturbances in adolescence. There is a small positive correlation between psychiatric impairment and IQ (r=0.10; p<0.05). This appears to be totally the result of a number of children seen for diagnosis of mental retardation whose psychiatric impairment was 0 or very low; when children with mental retardation are excluded, the correlation vanishes. A significant relationship (χ^2=37; p<0.01) also exists between psychiatric impairment and severity of EEG. This will be detailed under the section EEG. As will be seen, this probably relates to the correlation of EEG severity and mental retardation. The correlation between the Peterson-Quay score and psychiatric impairment has already been described.

TABLE 11

Distribution of Patients by IQ

Degree of Retardation	Number of Cases	Percent
0 = Normal IQ	837	79.3
1 = Highly scattered subtests*	37	3.5
2 = IQ 78 to 85	58	5.5
3 = IQ 68 to 77	59	5.6
4 = IQ 52 to 67	46	4.3
5 = IQ 36 to 51	12	1.1
6 = IQ 20 to 35	7	0.7
Total	1056	100.0

* On Wechsler Intelligence Scale for Children, marked discrepancy between Verbal and Performance IQ, one being greater than 85 and the other less than 78.

No relationship could be found between psychiatric impairment and (1) history of seizures; (2) difference between Verbal IQ and Performance IQ on the WISC.

IQ and Retardation

Although MBD is usually defined as a dysfunction of children with normal IQ, typical MBD symptoms are found in retarded children as well. Using several different instruments, but mainly the WISC, IQ measurements were available for 555 patients. The remainder were clearly, by clinical observation, of normal intelligence. Of 1056 patients, 124, or 12% were definitely retarded; 95, or 9% were borderline; and 837 or 79% were of normal intelligence. Detailed distribution is shown in Table 11. The average IQ for the entire patient group tested was 89, but if all children with IQ less than 80 are eliminated, the resulting average IQ is 97, a figure very close to the expected average of "normal" children. Because many patients are seen for the evaluation of mental retardation or slow learning, our population is heavily skewed to the retarded side, and we believed the segregation of retarded children in a separate group is justified. There is a significant correlation between IQ and (1) psychiatric impairment; (2) presence or absence of MBD (presence of MBD correlates with lower IQ scores); (3) presence or absence of "hard" neurological signs (presence of neurological signs correlates with lower IQ); (4) severity of EEG (more severe EEG abnormalities correlate with lower IQ). As mentioned earlier, the correlation with psychiatric impairment vanishes when retarded children are excluded. We do not conclude that retarded children have fewer psychiatric problems than the non-retarded, rather that our population is skewed to include a fairly large number of retarded children brought for intellectual rather than psychiatric evaluation.

Using the Wechsler Intelligence Scale for Children, the quantitative difference between Verbal IQ and Performance IQ, if large, is usually thought to be indicative of perceptual problems. In studies of patients whose right and left cerebral hemispheres were surgically disconnected by cutting the corpus callosum and other commissure structures, it was found that verbal tasks were largely confined to the left hemisphere, while the right hemisphere excelled in tasks such as spatial organization (Gazzaniga, 1967). Thus the WISC might give some clue as to the main areas of cerebral dysfunction, with left hemisphere dysfunction selectively lowering the Verbal IQ, right hemisphere dysfunction lowering the Performance IQ.

For 420 patients for whom WISC data are available, the difference between Verbal and Performance IQ ranged from +46 (Verbal higher than Performance) to —65 (Performance higher than Verbal), averaging —3, standard deviation 13. There were slightly more cases where the Performance IQ was higher than Verbal IQ than vice versa. In the standardization of the WISC (Seashore, 1950, 1951), in 50% of the cases the difference between Verbal and Performance IQ was 8 or more. For our non-MBD cases, 45% showed a difference of 8 or more. For MBD cases, the figure is 61%. For children diagnosed as having brain damage, it is 67%. This is consistent with the assumption that MBD is associated with perceptual defects which tend to increase the scatter of subtest results, since these subtests tap different aspects of thinking, some of which might be more affected than others by the brain dysfunction. The difference between Verbal and Performance IQ may not be the best measure of such scatter, but it does indicate some disparity between the two major types of thinking. In the extremes, a markedly depressed Verbal as opposed to Perfomance score would be labeled *aphasia,* and a depressed Performance as opposed to Verbal score, *apraxia.* Since most of school work involves verbal tasks and thinking, children with depressed verbal scores are more likely to have serious academic difficulties in school. However, children with depressed performance scores suffer in another way: their apraxia often goes unrecognized. Because they "sound" intelligent, and because on group IQ tests, which generally are highly biased to verbal accomplishments, they often get a fairly high score, they are considered "lazy" in school, and no further effort is made at investigating their low achievement.

In cross-correlating "Verbal minus Performance IQ" with other variables, we found no significant correlations, using both the algebraic and the absolute value of "Verbal minus Performance IQ."

The Electroencephalogram

The EEG control series, as explained in Chapter 2, used children especially selected by teachers as being "normal" children both academically and behaviorally. Our results are tabulated in Table 12, together with control data from other investigators.

Only 3.8% of our control children had any abnormality on the EEG, and the only abnormality found was 14/6 Hz positive spikes. For 100 children ages 6 to 12, three records were

Table 12

EEG Control Series

	Total Number of Children	Number with 14/6 Hz Positive Spikes	Number with Other Dysrhythmias	Total Abnormal
This Study	160	6 (3.8%)	0 (0%)	6 (3.8%)
Petersen et al. (1968)	757	Not stated	99 (13.1%)	Not stated
Lombroso et al. (1966)	212	58%	0 (0%)	(58%)
Gibbs and Gibbs (1963)	1176	21%	Not stated	Not stated
Kellaway et al. (1959)	1000	2.3%	Not stated	Not stated
Demerdash et al. (1968)	472	{ 35 (7.4%) definite { 32 (6.8%) questionable	Not stated	Not stated

abnormal—one each at ages 10, 11 and 12. For 60 children ages 13 to 18, three records were abnormal—one at age 13 and two at age 14; Gibbs and Gibbs (1964) mention a peak incidence at ages 10 to 14; our findings certainly correspond with theirs in this respect.

The series reported by Petersen (1968) and Demerdash (1968) are large; the children were carefully selected to avoid those with a history of prematurity, seizures, unconsciousness, paroxysmal headaches or abdominal pains, enuresis, encopresis, night terrors, and obvious physical disease; they were said to be "normal" in mental development, but they were apparently not carefully selected for absence of behavioral and learning problems as were the children in our control series, and this may explain the much higher incidence of EEG abnormalities they found. Kellaway (1959), in a much less carefully selected control series, found only 2.3% incidence of 14/6 Hz positive spikes.

It may be that no brain is entirely "normal," just as no skin is entirely free from blemishes; but, in so many areas of functioning, "perfect" cerebral integration is not critical, and only when integration is quantitatively impaired beyond a certain level, and in certain specific functions, can we find "symptoms" which we label "abnormal." Regardless of philosophical speculations on "normality," however, the fact remains that when control data are compared with the clinical findings on our patients, the difference is impressive. Only Lombroso (1966), in a study of all-night EEG records of boys at a residential school, found abnormalities at as high a frequency as our clinical findings. The weakness of his study derives from the well-known observation that boys at a residential school are much more apt to have behavior and learning problems than the average boy, for this is the most common reason, in our culture, for sending children to residential schools.

Because of the extreme care in which we chose our controls, we feel our results are highly significant clinically as well as statistically.

Of the 1056 *patients* examined, 568, or 53.8%, had an abnormal EEG. This is probably a low figure, as in 52 cases a sleep record (which brings out many abnormalities) was not obtainable. Even when retarded children are omitted, 431 of 837 patients, or 51.5%, had an abnormal EEG. Omitting all children with a history of having had even one seizure, the EEG was abnormal in 512 of 980, or 52.2%. Omitting all children with "hard" neurologic signs, an abnormal EEG was found in 538 of 1011, or 53.2%. In the presence of neurologic signs, the percentage of EEG abnormalities rose to 66.7%.*

Of the various types of EEG's the most common abnormality found was 14/6 Hz positive spikes, followed by abnormal fast records. The details are presented in Table 13 and Figure

---

* Data from another mental health center (Maine Township Mental Health Center, Park Ridge, Illinois) which routinely obtains an EEG as part of its work-up of children reveal the following statistics for a one-year period. Total patients, 84; 28 patients (33%) had 14/6 Hz positive spikes; 7 patients (8%) had other abnormalities; 44 patients (52%) had normal EEG awake and asleep, and 5 patients (6%) had a normal EEG awake only. This gives a total of 35 patients (42%) with definite EEG abnormalities. This figure is lower than for our series, but of the same order of magnitude. All of these EEG's were read by Dr. F. A. Gibbs.

TABLE 13

EEG Findings by Type of Abnormality

Type of EEG	Number	Percent
Normal awake and asleep	436	41.3
Normal awake only	52	4.9
6 Hz or 14/6 Hz positive spikes	226	21.4
6 Hz positive spike-waves	52	4.9
Fast waves	146	13.8
Negative and diphasic spikes	57	5.4
Negative spike-waves	39	3.7
Notched waves	4	0.4
Slow waves	15	1.4
Hyperventilation abnormality	4	0.4
Slow waves plus other abnormality	25	2.4
Total	1056	100.0

2. Illustrations of normal and abnormal EEG patterns are shown in Appendix G.

By somewhat arbitrarily grouping together the EEG findings according to the degree of severity of the EEG abnormality, as described on page 17, some correlations can be computed with other variables. The relationships between these variables and EEG are discussed below.

(1) Degree of retardation. Children with a normal IQ had an incidence of EEG abnormality of 51%; for retarded children with IQ 68 and over, 62% had an abnormal EEG; for retarded children with an IQ under 68, 63% had an abnormal EEG. Thus, retarded children of any degree of severity were more likely to have an abnormal EEG than children with a normal IQ ($\chi^2 = 8.4$; $p < 0.01$). From the data in Table 14, which tabulates degree of retardation versus severity of EEG, it can be seen that children with 6 Hz and 14/6 Hz positive spikes, 6 Hz positive spike-waves, and fast waves have about the same incidence of retardation as children with a normal EEG; while children with negative spikes, diphasic spikes, negative spike-waves, notched waves, and slow waves have

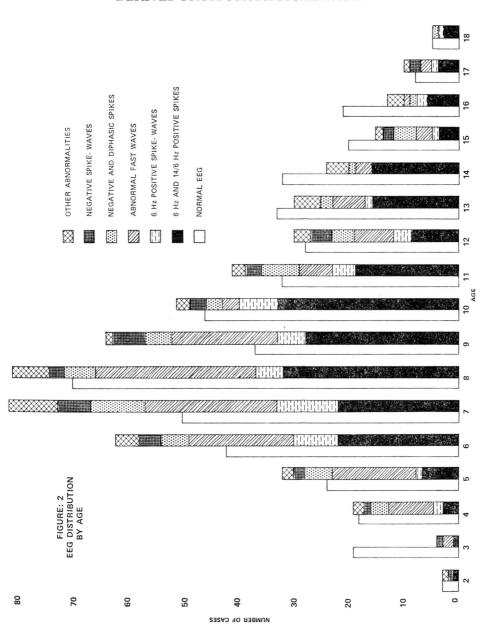

FIGURE: 2
EEG DISTRIBUTION
BY AGE

TABLE 14

Severity of EEG in Children with Normal IQ and with Varying Degree of Retardation

Degree of Retardation	Group I		Severity of EEG*—Number of Cases Group II		Group III		Group IV	
0	406	(83%)	338	(80%)	62	(65%)	31	(64%)
1, 2, 3	58	(12%)	61	(14%)	24	(25%)	11	(23%)
4, 5, 6	24	(5%)	25	(6%)	10	(10%)	6	(13%)
Total	488	(100%)	424	(100%)	96	(100%)	48	(100%)

(χ^2=21.7, p<0.01)

Group I: Normal EEG awake and asleep, plus normal EEG awake only.
Group II: 6 Hz and 14/6 Hz positive spikes, 6 Hz positive spike-waves, and abnormal fast waves.
Group III: Negative and diphasic spikes, negative spike-waves.
Group IV: Slow waves, notched waves, hyperventilation abnormalities, and slow waves plus other abnormalities.

TABLE 15

Severity of EEG in Children With and Without "Hard" Neurological Signs

	Group I		Severity of EEG*—Number of Cases Group II		Group III		Group IV	
No "hard" neurological signs	473	(93%)	405	(95%)	92	(96%)	41	(85%)
"Hard" neurological signs present	15	(7%)	19	(5%)	4	(4%)	7	(15%)
Total	488	(100%)	424	(100%)	96	(100%)	48	(100%)

(χ^2=14.3, p<0.01)

* Group I: Normal EEG awake and asleep, plus normal EEG awake only.
Group II: 6 Hz and 14/6 Hz positive spikes, 6 Hz positive spike-waves, and abnormal fast waves.
Group III: Negative and diphasic spikes, negative spike-waves.
Group IV: Slow waves, notched waves, hyperventilation abnormalities, and slow waves plus other abnormalities.

about double the incidence of retardation as children with a normal EEG (χ^2=21.7; p<0.01).

(2) *Presence of "hard" neurological signs.* Children with no "hard" neurological signs had an incidence of EEG abnormality of 53%, compared to 67% when "hard" neurological signs are present. From Table 15, it is apparent that

TABLE 16

Severity of EEG vs. Degree of Psychiatric Impairment in Children of Normal IQ Only

Psychiatric Impairment	Severity of EEG*—Number of Cases				
	Group I	Group II	Group III	Group IV	Total
0	15 (75%)	5 (25%)	0 (0%)	0 (0%)	20 (100%)
1	29 (56%)	21 (40%)	1 (2%)	1 (2%)	52 (100%)
2	102 (45%)	97 (43%)	22 (10%)	4 (2%)	225 (100%)
3	143 (48%)	126 (42%)	19 (6%)	9 (3%)	297 (99%)
4	65 (48%)	52 (39%)	10 (7%)	8 (6%)	135 (100%)
5	39 (49%)	24 (30%)	8 (10%)	8 (10%)	79 (99%)
6	13 (45%)	13 (45%)	2 (7%)	1 (3%)	29 (100%)

$(\chi^2 = 29.4, p < 0.05)$

* Group I: Normal EEG awake and asleep, plus normal EEG awake only.
Group II: 6 Hz and 14/6 Hz positive spikes, 6 Hz positive spike-waves, and abnormal fast waves.
Group III: Negative and diphasic spikes, negative spike-waves.
Group IV: Slow waves, notched waves, hyperventilation abnormalities, and slow waves plus other abnormalities.

neurological signs tended to be found in children in the most severe EEG category—mainly, slow waves and notched waves (χ^2=14.3; p<0.01). However, it should also be observed that many children with neurologic signs showed no EEG abnormality.

(3) *Psychiatric impairment.* The greater the psychiatric impairment, the more severe the EEG abnormality tended to be. Since it has already been demonstrated that retarded children have more frequent and more severe EEG abnormality, in Table 16 retarded children have been *excluded.* By inspecting the percentages given in Table 16, one can see clearly the association of greater psychiatric impairment with more severe EEG abnormalities (χ^2=29.4; p<0.05).

(4) *Clinical estimate of brain dysfunction.* Designating absence of any brain dysfunction as 0, minimal brain dysfunction as 1, and minimal brain dysfunction plus clinical psychiatric evidence of brain damage as 2, a marked relationship exists with severity of EEG (Table 17: χ^2=239, p<<0.0001).

(5) *Age.* Children older than 12 tended to have slightly fewer EEG abnormalities than younger age groups (Table 18; χ^2=14.7, p<0.02). This is in keeping with general knowledge that EEG abnormalities tend to improve with age. However, the incidence of the more severe EEG abnormalities did not vary with age. The 6 Hz and 14/6 Hz positive spikes were more common in the older age groups, as is generally reported in the literature (see Figure 2, page 41).

(6) *History of seizures.* Children with a history of seizures tended to have more severe EEG abnormalities (Table 19; χ^2=44.9, p<0.001). These data support the reports that 6 Hz and 14/6 Hz positive spikes and 6 Hz positive spike-waves are not associated with seizures (Gibbs and Gibbs, 1963). Table 20 arranges the same data in another way, revealing that with increasing frequency of seizures in a child's history the likelihood of having an abnormal EEG increases dramatically (χ^2=18.2, p<0.001).

TABLE 17

Severity of EEG vs. Clinical Estimate of Brain Dysfunction

Clinical Estimate of Brain Dysfunction	Severity of EEG*—Number of Cases				
	Group I	Group II	Group III	Group IV	Total
0 (absent)	204 (85%)	32 (13%)	2 (1%)	1 (½%)	239 (99½%)
1 (MBD)	245 (35%)	357 (51%)	75 (11%)	29 (4%)	706 (101%)
2 (MBD plus brain damage)	39 (35%)	35 (32%)	19 (17%)	18 (16%)	111 (100%)
Total	488	424	96	48	1056

($\chi^2 = 239$, $p << 0.001$)

* Group I: Normal EEG awake and asleep, plus normal EEG awake only.
Group II: 6 Hz and 14/6 Hz positive spikes, 6 Hz positive spike-waves, and abnormal fast waves.
Group III: Negative and diphasic spikes, negative spike-waves.
Group IV: Slow waves, notched waves, hyperventilation abnormalities, and slow waves plus other abnormalities.

TABLE 18
EEG Severity Grouped by Age

Age	Severity of EEG*—Number of Cases				Total
	Group I	Group II	Group III	Group IV	
2 to 6	106 (47%)	88 (39%)	22 (10%)	10 (4%)	226 (100%)
7 to 11	234 (42%)	249 (45%)	54 (10%)	19 (3%)	556 (100%)
12 to 18	148 (54%)	87 (32%)	20 (8%)	19 (7%)	274 (101%)
Total	488	424	96	48	1056

(χ^2=14.7, p<0.02)

* Group I: Normal EEG awake and asleep, plus normal EEG awake only.
Group II: 6 Hz and 14/6 Hz positive spikes, 6 Hz positive spike-waves, and abnormal fast waves.
Group III: Negative and diphasic spikes, negative spike-waves.
Group IV: Slow waves, notched waves, hyperventilation abnormalities, and slow waves plus other abnormalities.

TABLE 19
Severity of EEG in Children With and Without a History of Seizures

History of Seizures	Severity of EEG*—Number of Cases				Total
	Group I	Group II	Group III	Group IV	
No	468 (48%)	397 (41%)	75 (8%)	40 (4%)	980 (101%)
Yes	20 (26%)	27 (36%)	21 (28%)	8 (10%)	76 (100%)
Total	488	424	96	48	1056

(χ^2=44.9, p<0.001)

* Group I: Normal EEG awake and asleep, plus normal EEG awake only.
Group II: 6 Hz and 14/6 Hz positive spikes, 6 Hz positive spike-waves, and abnormal fast waves.
Group III: Negative and diphasic spikes, negative spike-waves.
Group IV: Slow waves, notched waves, hyperventilation abnormalities, and slow waves plus other abnormalities.

TABLE 20

Effect of Frequency of Seizures on Abnormality of EEG

	Normal EEG	Number of Cases Abnormal EEG	Total
Never had seizure	468 (48%)	512 (52%)	980 (100%)
Febrile seizures as infant	12 (36%)	21 (64%)	33 (100%)
Occasional non-febrile seizure	7 (30%)	16 (70%)	23 (100%)
Repeated seizures	1 (5%)	19 (95%)	20 (100%)
Total	488 (46%)	568 (54%)	1056 (100%)

$(\chi^2=18.2, p<0.001)$

There was no statistical relationship between severity of EEG and sex.

It should be noted that 162 patients had more than one EEG. General tendencies for an abnormal EEG to normalize with age, especially during adolescence, have been reported in the literature. However, sometimes a normal record at one time will be followed by an abnormal record a year or two later. This should not be surprising since it is well established that the conventional EEG taps only the outer centimeter of the cerebral cortex and is also only a limited time-sample of electrocortical activity; thus, the EEG is only a crude measure of true brain dysrhythmias.

In 11 cases, a 14/6 Hz positive spike record was followed later by an abnormally fast record, and for 10 cases, the reverse occurred. In four cases, negative spike waves, and in three cases, negative or diphasic spikes were followed in a subsequent record by 14/6 Hz positive spikes. This gives further credence to our belief that 14/6 Hz positive spikes have major clinical significance and should not be dismissed as of no consequence, as is the opinion of some electroencephalographers and clinicians. Appendix B lists a number of cases in which multiple EEG's were obtained and the nature of the changes.

In the 87 families where two or more children had MBD, the EEG findings were identical in the affected siblings in 18 cases (21%). Complete data on EEG findings in these children are found in Appendix C.

History of Seizures

This has been graded according to severity from 0 to 3 as described on page 17. The relationship between EEG and increasing frequency of seizures has already been demonstrated in the preceding section. The degree of retardation also has a small but positive correlation with frequency of seizures ($r=0.12$, $p<0.001$). IQ also relates inversely with the frequency of seizures ($\chi^2=8.3$, $p<0.05$)—the lower the IQ, the more likely the child has had seizures. Children with clinical evidence of brain damage have a higher incidence of seizures than children with only MBD, and the latter have a higher incidence of seizures than children without MBD ($r=0.14$, $p<0.001$). No statistical relationship exists between a history of seizures and (1) degree of psychiatric impairment; (2) sex; (3) Peterson-Quay score; (4) age.

Family Data

The 1056 cases represent only 951 families, the difference being due to the presence of more than one child-patient in 105 families. Appendix C summarizes the data on siblings represented in the study. In a number of families, it was noted that all of the boys had MBD whereas none of the girls did. In some families, every child had MBD.

Twin Data

Of the families where more than one child was represented, five involved patients who were twins: in two cases, both twins were brought as patients; and in three cases, one twin was the patient and the co-twin was seen only for research purposes. Of the twins seen, all were monozygotic by history and clinical examination (no attempt was made to verify monozygocity by laboratory study except in one case). In two sets of twins, both twins were diagnosed as having MBD, although their dysfunctions were not identical, but were more severe in one co-twin than the other. Detailed histories are presented in Chapter 7 (Cases #442-443, page 126, and #1011-1012, page 115). In one set of twins, one twin was clearly MBD. The other was probably MBD—the family moved before the co-twin could be completely examined. In the remaining two sets, one twin had MBD while the co-twin did not. In these two sets, the co-twins with MBD had abnormal EEG's, the co-twins without MBD had normal EEG's. One of these sets is Case #583 described on page 110. Detailed EEG data are listed in Appendix D.

Obstetric History and Unusual Medical Histories

Obstetric histories as given by parents are notoriously unreliable, and it was beyond the scope of our study to obtain data from physicians, which would be more reliable. However, our general impression is that obstetric complications were not involved in the great majority of MBD patients. There were at least 9 prematures (birth weight less than five pounds), two of whom were less than three pounds. One mother had taken Thalidomide during pregnancy, and her son had typical defects of the limbs. He also had typical symptoms of MBD. Another child with typical MBD symptoms had galactosemia diagnosed almost immediately after birth and was treated with diet. Intellectually, he was within the average IQ range. Still another child had an obscure aminoaciduria. She was not at first retarded but was unable to concentrate at all, and her IQ scores gradually deteriorated.*

---

* Kalyanaraman (1972) reported on hyperkinesis in two children with maple syrup urine disease (keto-aciduria).

One of the adolescent patients had an XXY chromosomal abnormality (Klinefelter's syndrome). His EEG showed 14/6 Hz positive spikes. Behaviorally, he was extremely explosive and aggressive.*

There was one case of precocious puberty at age 8 with typical MBD symptoms; two cases with a history of maternal rubella during the first trimester of pregnancy; one case of carbon monoxide poisoning; two cases of erythroblastosis fetalis; two cases of microcephaly; one child with brain damage due to cardiac arrest, another due to severe head injury, another with brain damage due to birth injury, another with brain damage due to cerebral hemorrhage. Ten children had histories of severe malnutrition in infancy.

Psychiatric Syndromes

The great bulk of our patients came for behavior problems, learning problems, or both. In investigating the 132 cases with more serious problems (5 or 6 on the scale of psychiatric impairment), we found the following:

1. Behavior Problems	67	(51%)
2. Behavior and Learning Problems	23	(17%)
3. Retardation with Behavior Problems	19	(14%)
4. Retardation with Neurosis	1	(1%)
5. Psychosis		
a. Autism	4	(3%)
b. Childhood Schizophrenia	8	(6%)
c. Other Psychosis	3	(2%)
6. Neurosis		
a. Anxiety	2	(2%)
b. Depression	2	(2%)
7. Learning Problem with Aphasia	3	(2%)

* See also Gardner and Neu (1972).

Of the psychoses, one child diagnosed as childhood schizophrenia had typical MBD symptoms as well; the seven others diagnosed as childhood schizophrenia did not have MBD symptoms. In contrast, the autistic and other psychotic children all had MBD or frank brain damage.

One of the depressed patients had MBD and learning problems; he was the only suicide in our series.

4

The Natural History of Minimal Brain Dysfunction

Onset

It is appropriate to review the course of MBD in childhood. Sometimes hyperactivity is present before birth; a number of mothers have remarked that the fetus was unusually active in utero. At times the newborn child is described as unusually restless. In severe cases, sleep is of short duration and the parents complain that the child is awake for unusual lengths of time. Colic is a fairly common complaint the first three to six months of life. We do not, unfortunately, have quantitative data, but our impression is that colic is not infrequently a forerunner of the usual MBD syndrome. Headbanging and rocking are frequently mentioned; these seem to be early symptoms of hyperkinesis. As a child reaches age two, the definitive signs of MBD may become apparent, but this is true only of the more severe cases. For mild cases, it is difficult to distinguish between an active 2-year-old and a hyperactive one. One crucial difference is the attention span: even the very active child of two can concentrate on some plaything he likes, but a child that age who wanders from one thing to another at intervals of only a few seconds is likely to have MBD. A mother who has had several children may be quite perspicacious in distinguishing the affected child from the other children by the quality of their play.

For children manifesting only learning problems, it is unusual for any concern to be shown before school age, since concentrated formal teaching is rarely attempted before that time. For behavior problems or problems with concentration, difficulties may be noted earlier in more severe cases, but for milder problems it is much more common for the school teacher to be the first one to express concern. This is understandable if one remembers, as has been mentioned earlier, that one-to-one situations or small groups may impose no stress on an MBD child; the school setting, requiring sitting still and attending to complex tasks, is much more stressful and, therefore, much more likely to elicit symptoms. Alert nursery school teachers may also pick up MBD in fairly mild cases, but for the most part, it is the first or second grade teacher who is most likely to be concerned about the child's behavior. This is reflected in the modal age of 8 for the children we examined. This is not to imply that parents see no problems in these children; they often do and one-fourth of our children, as mentioned earlier, were referred by the family. But for many cases, it is apparent that difficulties in school are recognized more quickly than difficulties at home.

Typical case

A typical history is demonstrated in the following case.

Donald is 7, referred by the school because of extreme restlessness. When he first started kindergarten, he was so restless that his mother was persuaded to keep him home for about a year. The following year he attended kindergarten and adjusted marginally; the current year, in first grade, has been very difficult. His teacher writes, "He is constantly trying to get a reaction from people. His mother is not pleased with the school situation. She feels that Donald has never had trouble in school until this year, and that I am picking on him. As well as getting into trouble in the classroom, Donald has created problems in the lunchroom and on the bus. The bus driver is not able to handle him, and it is very difficult for the lunchroom supervisors.

"Donald is a very bright boy—above average. He reads and does all oral work with ease. He avoids written work completely but asks questions about it all of the time, so that you are sure he is accomplishing something. Arithmetic tends to give him a little trouble, only because it takes time.

"Socially Donald is tolerated more than accepted. He wants to be a leader in everything and is often ignored by the other children. He feels he is very important, that he can do what he wants. Donald's coordination for printing is very poor. Although it has improved greatly since the beginning of the year, he still has many reversals. He avoids all written work whenever possible. Many different things have been tried in my room to help Donald this year. Nothing has worked. He talks to everyone. To Donald, there is no such thing as a stranger. If you talk to Donald about his behavior, he will try to change the subject. If you stop him from doing something he shouldn't, he will listen to you until another person appears, and then he will start to scream and yell. Often he is rude in his comments if he has an audience. He loves to watch people react to his behavior, either negative or positive.

"I have tried to get help for Donald since the first week of school and feel that I have received none; however, I have been told that Donald has been observed and is not a problem. This is true *only* if you are working with him on an individual basis. When he is one of 31 children as he was in the beginning of the year, things can get very difficult.

"As far as Donald's behavior goes, he has no self-control. He will get the attention of the teacher in charge no matter where he is by yelling or pulling on them. He also has trouble when he is on the playground because he has no idea of how to play with the other children. I feel that unless he gets some kind of help soon, things are going to continue to get worse."

In the questionnaire, mother checked the following items *"Yes, very much"*: crying over minor annoyances and hurts; preoccupation; jealousy over attention paid other children; short attention span; inattentiveness to what others say; hypersensitivity; laziness in school; tension; disobedience; uncooperativeness in group situations; poor muscle coordination; hyperactivity; negativeness; and excessive talking.

Early history was entirely uneventful. An EEG revealed a right temporal focus of 14/6 Hz positive spiking.

In the interview with the psychiatrist, he was charming, pleasant, extremely open and verbal, but quite fidgety. When asked what animal he would choose if he had to be an animal, he would be a cobra because they are one of the most poisonous of snakes. When asked what he would wish for if he could have three magic wishes, he wished for three billion dollars, to travel all over the world, and to have a lion as a pet. When asked to draw, he drew extremely hastily and carelessly as though trying to get the task over in record time. Yet, it was very obvious that he was a very bright child by the type of questions he asked, by the many observations he made, and by the logical turn of his mind in discussing things that he saw in the office.

Many MBD children are seen as immature. It is easy to assume psychogenic immaturity, but neurologic deficits may be more important (Case #626, page 132). Accident proneness is common. This has been reported before (Husband and Hinton, 1972); our data confirm this, though we cannot quantify this. Frequently when there is only one MBD child among several normal children, the MBD child becomes the scapegoat for everything. Case #499, page 58, illustrates this well.

It was quite common to find fathers totally denying any problem with their MBD child. Occasionally they would withdraw their child from treatment. A number of mothers brought their children surreptitiously—not wanting the father to know about it for fear he would sabotage treatment. These mothers thus had to cope not only with their child's problem by themselves, but also with their husband's denial of any difficulty. Fathers sometimes would see their child simply as "bad" and in need of punishment, whereas this was rare with mothers.

Foster children who had extremely traumatic experiences with their natural parents presented unusually severe problems. Whether MBD resulted from genetic causes or from malnutrition or head trauma was hard to determine, but sometimes the impression was gained that the child had been abused by their natural parents partly *because* he was difficult and unresponsive to the usual measures.

For many children, development was described as perfectly normal for several years, usually up to age three or four, at which time the MBD symptoms appeared to begin.

Course and Follow-Up

There are not many follow-up studies of MBD in the literature. The longest follow-up, 25 years, concentrates on neurologic findings, and there are few data on psychiatric outcomes (Menkes et al. 1967).

In describing the outcome of untreated MBD, we are relying on two sources: (1) the history of relatives of patients who by description had typical MBD symptoms themselves; and (2) a follow-up of patients seen at the Center diagnosed as MBD but not treated, usually because of lack of parental cooperation or interest.

Many parents have indicated that one of them, or a grandfather, or an uncle had identical symptoms to the patient when he or she was young (Mendelson, 1971; Morrison and Stewart, 1971). The symptomatology can be divided in two categories: primarily learning problems or primarily behavior problems. Those parents who described learning problems in themselves usually reported a marked residual deficit in their education, usually in reading, often in spelling, less often in arithmetic. Nevertheless, they were generally successful in their field and saw their deficit as a handicap but not as a disability. Some had curtailed their education by dropping out of school after grammar school or some time in high school. Others had gone on to college and pushed their way through despite their handicap. Of course, ours is a highly biased sample since those who had become unsuccessful would be less likely to find themselves as upper-lower class or middle-class parents bringing their child in for help.

The story is somewhat different for those who had behavior problems when young. The sample is biased here, too, toward more successful outcomes, but these parents describe major adjustment difficulties when they grew up. "My parents thought I was headed for St. Charles [an institution for delinquent boys]. I never studied and just raised hell all the time, but somehow by the time I was 18, I had developed some sense and settled down. I had trouble getting into college because of my grades. Once in college, I really worked." This man is now an airline pilot. Another airline pilot: "I guess I was impossible when I was a kid. My mother put me in [a therapeutic school for disturbed children] for several years. I had it rough as an adolescent, but then I seemed to have gotten myself together."

Quite often a boy was described by his mother as "just like his father." These fathers were not infrequently absent, either divorced, separated, or in prison. Some were alcoholics.

In general, the impression is that the great majority of parents who presumably had MBD as a child "made it" and those who did not were in the minority, but for those in this minority, the consequences could be severe. It is hard to escape the conclusion that in these cases MBD played a crucial role in their downfall. It takes little imagination to see how impulsiveness, if unchecked, could lead to serious difficulties. A case in point is the following:

Cases #499 and #499A—Father and Son Both with MBD Associated with Violence

Mr. J. Z. was 41 at the time of his referral from the Department of Children and Family Services on the complaint that he severely beat up his son, Keith, who at the time was 13. This boy had angered him and he beat him steadily for about twenty minutes, when his wife finally called the police. He had beaten up this boy many times in the past and had also beaten up his wife, who on one occasion had attempted suicide with a large number of diet pills and was in a coma for a day. According to the social worker from the Division of Children and Family Services, "The home is extremely pathological. All the families in the neighborhood keep away from this family. There are eight children, and an 11-year-old boy is unable to read or write because he blocks out the teachers, and the 6-year-old girl is afraid to attend school and has been permitted to stay home."

The psychiatrist who saw Mr. Z. found him a short, wiry, pleasant-looking man, who seemed quite friendly and likeable, and who seemed to want to do the right thing. He has been working 84 hours a week to support his family of eight children. *His* father was described as hot-headed and domineering, ruling the family with an iron hand. He had a lot of trouble with his father, but he did respect him. He was always getting into trouble; he did poorly in school, but could handle jobs well. He said things would not be so bad if he did not have to worry so much about his relationship with Keith. He knows Keith does not like him and is rebelling against him. He feels bad about beating him up. He says when he gets angry, he doesn't know what he is doing and almost killed Keith on one occasion.

During World War II he was in the armed services, was very quick-tempered, and had a number of contacts with psychiatrists.

An EEG revealed generalized paroxysmal 6 Hz positive spike-waves awake and in drowsiness.

A few weeks later, the social worker made a home visit to discuss family relationships and what could be done about them. Mr. Z. complained that he was being hemmed in by the Mental Health Center and by Children and Family Services and had been reduced to simply being the breadwinner. He wanted to control the discipline in the family and thought no one should be allowed to tell him what to do. While he was talking, the social worker reported that he began to turn white, and as he got angrier and angrier, he became "white as a dead person" and ran from one part of the house to the other as though he had gone crazy. Finally he regained his composure and his color came back.

Despite efforts at psychotherapy, family counseling and pharmacotherapy, the situation with Mr. Z. did not improve. He and his wife finally agreed that divorce would be the only answer, and this took place several months later.

The son, Keith, had been in difficulty in school ever since kindergarten and more recently in trouble with the law. He is the only child that his father had become rather extremely violent with, although, as mentioned before, his father had also been violent with his mother. He was a slow learner and had been retained in the second grade. His behavior had deteriorated to such an extent that he spent most of his time in the principal's office. A recent WISC revealed a Verbal IQ of 87; Performance IQ, 113; Full Scale IQ, 99. His lowest score among the subtests was on a test of comprehension, where he demonstrated very poor social judgment.

Keith was 13 when seen by the psychiatrist at the Mental Health Center. He was friendly, cooperative, displayed no anxiety. He appeared to relate well but seemed not to be truthful and tended to place responsibility for any problems on anyone but himself. He did not display very much hostility to his father, and actually seemed to defend his father's behavior. In general, the behavior during the interview was marked by a great deal of denial.

An EEG revealed in drowsiness and sleep a right temporal focus of 14/6 Hz positive spiking with frequent occipital spread.

Both father and son were diagnosed as having brain dysfunction. Before any therapeutic program could be begun, however, the family came totally apart. Keith got into increasing difficulty in school, eventually stole a car, and was sentenced to a center for delinquent children.

As is the case in our sample of children, adults who reported MBD symptoms when they were young were predominently male but not always. Two families where the mothers were involved are of special interest, Case #1011, page 115, and Case #63A below.

Case #63A—MBD Symptoms in Mother and Three Children

This 38-year-old woman had never been a good student. She could not use language well, especially to express herself. She did finish high school and became a dancer, eventually opening a school of dance at which she was quite successful. The business part of the school, however, she had to leave to her husband because she could never handle it adequately. In listening to this woman, her expressive dysphasia was very apparent. She talked in short, disconnected phrases, frequently flitting from one thought to another with no connecting bridge. She gave the superficial appearance of being scatter-brained because of the staccato, disorganized speech, yet it was clear that she was an intelligent, thoughtful woman.

She had a younger brother who had a similar language problem but with more emphasis on receptive rather than expressive disorder. He was interviewed also. He had a limited vocabulary, had dropped out of school because of severe reading problems, and was somewhat explosive and impulsive. He worked as a truck driver, but complained that he frequently made mistakes in his work because of inadequate concentration.

The woman had three sons, all of whom had a mild hyperkinetic syndrome; all were on medication and doing very well. One child had a reading problem and needed special academic help; one was a good student (after medication); and the third was an excellent student. She was persuaded to undertake a double blind experiment with imipramine, 50 mg, twice daily. The active medication led to considerable improvement in the disorganization, both verbally, which could be detected by outsiders, and in terms of feeling "better put together."

The other case was a woman who had four children, all with MBD, and who reported feeling totally disorganized on awakening in the morning, unable to remember things, get the children off to school properly, or think things out until several hours had elapsed. She, too, improved considerably with imipramine, reporting that she now felt "like a human being" when she awoke. This is Case #1011, described more fully on page 117.

To get another picture of the natural history of MBD, we followed up 33 cases that had been worked up and diagnosed as MBD but who were never treated with medication, or with any other modality. The cases are divided into 13 with learning problems predominantly, and 20 with behavior problems predominantly.

The 13 children, when first seen for learning problems, averaged 8.3 years in age, and when followed up averaged 15.2 years of age, almost a seven-year average follow-up. All were reported doing well. Some had been retained a grade; some had been put in special classes; only one had had an abnormal EEG; three were mildly retarded. Many had large discrepancies between Verbal IQ and Performance IQ on the WISC.

The 20 children with behavioral problems had an average age of 9.5 when first seen, and 16.3 when followed up, again almost a seven-year average follow-up. Four were girls; sixteen were boys. In rating their progress on a five-point scale, the following were the outcomes: doing very well, 6 children; doing well, 3 children; doing fair, 6 children; doing poorly, 2 children; doing very poorly, 4 children. Three of the latter were, or had been, in prison, and one was a girl married to a ne'er-do-well twice her age. Three of these four had had abnormal EEG's, one with a history of seizures, and these same three were also mildly retarded (IQ's 75, 73 and 77).

A typical history is selected from each group. *Case #748 is a behavior problem now doing very well.* This patient was 14 when first seen because of constant rebelliousness, defiance, hostility and impulsiveness. Academically he did well. He would not speak during the interview and was thoroughly defiant to all he encountered. A year later he was sent to the Youth Home for car theft. By the next year, his behavior softened. He finished school and is now 19 and doing a good job at work. His mother stated, "He outgrew his mischief."

Case #829 illustrates a behavior disorder now doing well. This 5-year-old boy was brought in for temper, defiance, meanness and hyperactivity. His father was unusually punitive. By age 9, he had gradually settled down and was now doing well for the first time since beginning school.

Case #199 is a behavior disorder now doing fair. This patient was 9 when first seen for complaints of underachievement, babyishness, impulsiveness and passive-aggressiveness.

His IQ was 87. He continued to do poorly in school and dropped out in tenth grade. He was then sent to a school to study carpet-laying, and now at age 22 works at this trade steadily. He has few friends but does have a girlfriend. He is frequently moody and irritable.

Case #822 is a behavior disorder and learning disorder now doing poorly. This boy was 8 when first examined because of explosiveness, fire-setting, not being able to sit still, getting into everything. He frequently read backwards. Follow-up at age 14 revealed that he does poorly in school, is not learning much in a regular classroom, and is in frequent conflict with his teacher.

Case #785 is a behavior disorder now doing very poorly. This boy was 14 when first seen because of lying, stealing, cruelty to animals and lack of interest in school. His WISC score was Verbal IQ, 98; Performance IQ, 83. Academically, his achievement was fair. He had been a premature infant and had numerous spells of unconsciousness as an infant. During the ensuing years, he was in many difficulties including involvement in illicit drugs and burglaries. He spent time at the state mental hospital, Youth Home, and in prison. He is now 22.

Although our sample is small because long-term follow-up turned up very few who had not moved away, we can conclude with some assurance that for children with mainly learning problems, the outlook for a good life adjustment is excellent. When behavior problems are the primary complaint, about half do well; a fourth, fair; and a fourth, poor. This outcome is exactly identical to the outcome of 83 children followed up by Mendelson et al. (1971). Their follow-up averaged 3½ years, or half the average follow-up of our data.

5

Types of Therapy Used

The treatment of MBD children consisted of three major
modalities:

A. Pharmacotherapy of children
B. Counseling of parents
C. Counseling of teachers

The latter was of considerable importance since many of the
children, by the nature of the illness, exhibited many more
problems in school than at home.

For pharmacotherapy, we divided the drugs used into three
categories:

A. Brain catecholamine enhancers

1. Stimulants

a. D-amphetamine (Dexedrine)
b. R-amphetamine (Benzedrine)
c. Methylphenidate (Ritalin)

2. Non-stimulants

    a. Tricylic Amines

        1. Imipramine (Tofranil, Presamine)
        2. Desipramine (Norpramin, Pertofrane)
        3. Amitriptyline (Elavil)
        4. Nortriptyline (Aventyl)
        5. Protriptyline (Vivactyl)

    b. MAO Inhibitors

        1. Isocarboxazid (Marplan)

B. Anti-convulsants

    1. Diphenylhydantoin (Dilantin)
    2. Methsuximide (Celontin)
    3. Ethosuximide (Zarontin)
    4. Acetazolamide (Diamox)

C. Major tranquilizers

    1. Phenothiazines

        a. Chlorpromazine (Thorazine)
        b. Thioridazine (Mellaril)
        c. Thiothixene (Navane)

    2. Butyrophenones

    Haloperidol (Haldol)

In general, the third category, the major tranquilizers, were not chosen unless the other two did not succeed, since the tranquilizers are more apt to generally slow down functioning whereas the other two seem to work more physiologically as though "normalizing" behavior rather than suppressing motor activity. The first category, the catecholamine enhancers, were our first choice, and among these the stimulants were somewhat preferred because more is known about their pharmacology and they have been in use for longer periods of time. However, since further experience has convinced us of the effectiveness and low toxicity of the tricyclic amines, we have used more imipramine and desipramine. The other tricyclics appear to have greater number of side effects and were used only rarely. The MAO inhibitors were found to have a major side effect of orthostatic hypotension, which has discouraged their use.

Among the anti-convulsants, diphenylhydantoin was the first choice because of lack of sedation. The presence of negative or diphasic spikes or of spike-waves on the EEG was generally an indication for using anti-convulsants, but children who did not show these EEG patterns and who did not respond to catecholamine enhancers were also given a trial of anti-convulsants. Of course, some children with epilepsy were already receiving anti-convulsants, which presumably had not fully controlled the MBD symptoms. These children were then tried on stimulants or tricyclic amines in addition to the anti-convulsants.

None of the children was given formal psychotherapy. Counseling with the parents consisted of interviews in which the nature of MBD was explained and management techniques using structure, prevention, supervision and firmness were encouraged. Details of this type of counseling will be found in Chapter 10. For selected mothers, group therapy was provided, usually when mothers felt unusually inadequate or the children were unusually difficult to manage. Counseling with the teachers and other school personnel consisted of staff conferences, telephone conversations, written reports, lecture and discussion groups, and pamphlets.

Occasionally, for children with poor muscle coordination, we recommend coordination exercises (Appendix E). Some authorities place great emphasis on coordination exercises, believing that it helps not only muscular coordination, but also reading and other cerebral functions. We have no data on which to judge this. Any program of coordination exercises, unless pushed to an extreme, has the virtue of being simple, inexpensive, and harmless; it is certainly beneficial to counteract clumsiness and ungainliness.

At the time of writing, there is considerable interest in "megavitamin" therapy. None of our patients had this treatment.

6

Efficacy of Therapy

By using the placebo phase as a reference point, we are convinced the major factor for improvement was the medication used. By employing the placebo first, the psychological effect of the diagnostic process, which would be expected to be greater initially and fade after a time, was maximized for the placebo and minimized for other medications. Essentially, the study was "double blind," for parents who reported changes did not know what medications were used, and teachers who reported changes often did not know when the medications were altered or sometimes even that medications were being tried. Thus, the essential decision of improvement or lack of improvement coming from parents and teachers, rather than primarily from our own observations, rendered this study quite similar to a double blind procedure. However, it must be kept in mind that the placebo and medication periods were not comparable in some respects; for example, the sequence of administration was almost always placebo first and active medication afterward, and the time of observation

TABLE 21

Placebo Results

Effect of Placebo	Number of Cases	Percent	
+5 = Almost complete remission of symptoms	0	0	
+4 = Excellent improvement	1	0.2	
+3 = Good improvement	0	0	
+2 = Some significant improvement	3	0.5	
+1 = Very mild improvement	23	3.7 ⎤	
0 = No change whatsoever	571	92.4 ⎬ 98.7	
—1 = Slightly worse	16	2.6 ⎦	
—2 = Definitely worse	4	0.6	
	618	100.0	

Average effect of placebo = +0.01

was relatively short—one to two weeks—compared to active medications.

Placebo Effects

Of 618 patients given placebo, 98.7% reported no change or only very mild changes, leaving only 1.3% with significant reactions to placebo. The complete results are given in Table 21. Using the improvement rating shown in the table, the average improvement on placebo was 0.01.

Compared to the usual psychiatric patient, the percent of non-reactors to placebo was remarkably high. Even with the very strict interpretation of a non-reactor as one who reported (parents' and teachers' observations) *no change whatsoever,* the percent of non-reactors was 92.4, which is still extremely high. Put another way, only 7.6% reported even the slightest change with placebo. Typical remarks made by observers were: "it didn't do a thing;" "no real change;" "nothing;" "we really couldn't tell any difference." A review of placebo effect (Kurland, 1960) indicates that for 1082 patients in 15 studies, 35% showed a positive effect from placebo. Some of the reports that the child became worse with placebo could be traced to symptoms of intercurrent illness, such as flu or a cold, which the reporter had attributed to the placebo. Other reports that the child was somewhat worse could be traced to disruption in the household, such as mother being sick or away from home.

In investigating cases reported considerably worse or considerably better on placebo, we found one 9-year-old girl who was considered to have an *excellent improvement* with placebo, an improvement which was maintained over a year's time. This 9-year-old girl had an IQ of 65. She was brought to the Center because not only was she slow in school, but she seemed to be off in a world of her own. She reacted poorly to all active medication but on placebo she seemed to thrive. When the placebo was discontinued, her behavior deteriorated. The placebo was, therefore, continued for over a year with continued improvement in her functioning. Aside from the observation that this was a rather dependent girl, no explanation could be found for this response to placebo.

There were three other children who responded with *some significant improvement* to placebo. In two of these cases, the mother was convinced that there was something wrong with the child and was quite aggressive and pushing toward him, while the father was passive and convinced there was nothing wrong. The third child was a retarded child and also a foster child; the foster mother seemed largely unaware of his problems and was probably unable to give an accurate picture of change with medication.

There were four children who reported *definitely worse* on placebo. One was a foster child whose foster mother was quite disinterested in coming to the Mental Health Center but had been pressured by the school. She withdrew this child rather rapidly. Another child with a school phobia was very frightened by the diagnostic workup and was abetted in this by her mother's providing inappropriate sympathy for her child's fears. This child did respond to a moderate degree to meth-

TABLE 22

Double Blind Control Study of Six Children

Control	Medication Used	Response to Medication	Response to Placebo
A	d-amphetamine 10 mg time capsule	Irritable, cranky	None
B	d-amphetamine 10 mg time capsule	Touchy, cried easily	None
C	d-amphetamine 10 mg time capsule	None	None
D	Methylphenidate 10 mg AM and noon	None	None
E	Methylphenidate 10 mg AM and noon	Irritable, touchy	None
F	Methylphenidate 10 mg AM and noon	None	None

ylphenidate and also to d-amphetamine. The third child who was reported considerably worse from placebo also was brought in by his mother under pressure. His mother was upset by the workup and was generally overprotective. Later, the child and mother were given psychotherapy. The fourth child was a mildly retarded child; all of the medications, including placebo, were reported to have bad effects, despite the fact that he had typical MBD symptoms.

Pharmacotherapy of Children without Evidence of Minimal Brain Dysfunction

Thirteen children who were clinically diagnosed as not having MBD were nevertheless treated with medications—five with methylphenidate, four with d-amphetamine, and four with des/imipramine. All of these patients were siblings of MBD patients whose parents thought they had somewhat similar problems. After the diagnostic workup none of these children was considered MBD and none of them had abnormal EEG's. The average improvement rating for the thirteen

TABLE 23

Average Improvement for Medications Used
Six Months or Longer

Definitive Medication Used	Dosage Range	No. of Patients	Average Number of Years Treated	Average Improvement
Methylphenidate	5 to 140 mg/day	287	2.43	2.88
D-amphetamine	2½ to 40 mg/day	231	2.37	2.59
Des/Imipramine	10 to 350 mg/day	74	2.36	2.97
Others		30	3.08	1.93

children was —0.15, that is, most were judged slightly worse with medications (these data are included in Table 25).

In addition, six children, asymptomatic brothers of patients who had MBD, were asked to volunteer as controls. The medications were administered in double blind fashion; the results are given in Table 22. Also, two asymptomatic boys, ages 8 and 10, both with normal EEG's, were given d-amphetamine in a 10 mg time capsule, methylphenidate, 20 mg, and placebo. Both responded to the d-amphetamine by becoming slightly "high;" one was slightly irritable with methylphenidate, and neither had any effect from placebo.

Thus, no control showed any calming or settling effects from active medication.

The following variables were investigated but showed no correlation with placebo reactions:

1. Degree of psychiatric impairment
2. Type of EEG
3. Presence or absence of MBD
4. Sex

Active Medications

Using active medications, the overall improvement averaged 2.74 for all drugs—corresponding to "good improve-

TABLE 24

Results of Treatment of MBD Children with Medication Six Months or Longer

Degree of Improvement	Methylphenidate	D-amphetamine	Number of Cases Des/Imipramine	Others	Total
5	45 (16%)	36 (16%)	11 (15%)	1 (3%)	93 (15%)
4	73 (25%)	46 (20%)	19 (26%)	3 (10%)	141 (23%)
3	81 (28%)	57 (25%)	18 (24%)	7 (23%)	163 (26%)
2	38 (13%)	29 (13%)	16 (22%)	8 (27%)	91 (15%)
1	9 (3%)	15 (6%)	4 (5%)	4 (13%)	32 (5%)
0	26 (9%)	40 (17%)	5 (7%)	7 (23%)	78 (12%)
−1	12 (4%)	5 (2%)	1 (1%)	0 (0%)	18 (3%)
−2	3 (1%)	3 (1%)	0 (0%)	0 (0%)	6 (1%)
	287 (99%)	231 (100%)	74 (100%)	30 (99%)	622 (100%)

TABLE 25

Results of Treatment for Cases of MBD Absent, MBD Present, and MBD Present Together With Clinical Evidence of Brain Damage

	Methylphenidate	D-amphetamine	Average Improvement Des/Imipramine	Others	Total
MBD Absent	0.40 (5 pts.)	−0.75 (4 pts.)	−0.25 (4 pts.)	—	−0.15 (13 pts.)
MBD Present	2.99 (248 pts.)	2.73 (202 pts.)	3.22 (67 pts.)	1.99 (20 pts.)	2.88 (537 pts.)
MBD plus Brain Damage	2.44 (34 pts.)	2.32 (25 pts.)	1.25 (3 pts.)	1.81 (10 pts.)	2.26 (72 pts.)

ment." Improvement for the various drugs, all used an average of 2.4 years, is listed in Table 23. Results of treatment, separated by the *degree* of improvement, are given in Table 24.

If degree of improvement from 2 to 5 is considered clinically significant, then it can be seen that 78% of all treated MBD patients improved significantly. For patients taking methylphenidate, this figure is 83%; for d-amphetamine, 73%; for des/imipramine, 86%; for others, 63%. It would appear from these tables that imipramine and desipramine are the medications of choice, followed by methylphenidate and d-amphetamine. However, this interpretation is not correct. *It must be emphasized that each child was given the drug which, on exploratory testing, appeared to work best.* The data do show, however, that methylphenidate, d-amphetamine and des/imipramine are very effective medications for MBD. On the other hand, when these medications do not help and others, mainly diphenylhydantoin, thioridazine, and haloperidol are used, the results are not nearly as good. It is likely that these figures would be higher if patient cooperation were optimum. Sometimes parents are not willing to explore a variety of medications when the first one does not work as well as anticipated.* Occasionally a child did best on a combination of des/imipramine with methylphenidate or with d-amphetamine. This may be due to the effect of des/imipramine in enhancing the blood level of the stimulants and vice versa (Perel et al. 1969).

The following variables show some correlation with treatment results:

1. *Presence or absence of MBD as diagnosed clinically* (shown in Table 25). The data on "MBD Absent" result from attempts to treat such patients with medication despite the clinical impression in order to learn more about response

---

* Data from patients seen in private practice indicate that one can expect significant clinical improvement in close to 95% of MBD cases.

to medications. Clearly children clinically diagnosed as not having MBD were no better, or slightly worse, when treated with drugs; whereas, the overall improvement in MBD children averaged somewhat less than "good improvement." It should be noted that all treated cases involve treatment of at least half a year. In cases treated a shorter period of time, it was found that some non-MBD patients improved with medication. Des/imipramine has some sedative effect initially, and so some children were "tranquilized" for a period of time. A rare reaction to the stimulants was an increase in energy and a greater accomplishment of tasks, similar to an adult reaction to stimulants. These effects did not last longer than a few weeks, however. By limiting these data to children treated more than six months, we have eliminated all transient effects.

2. *Degree of Brain Dysfunction.* Those children whose brain dysfunction appeared particularly severe and who exhibited actual clinical evidence of brain damage (bizarreness, perseveration, autism, aphasia, severe speech defects) showed poorer results from treatment, with an overall improvement of 2.26, as opposed to an average improvement of 2.88 for MBD without clinical evidence of brain damage. Even so, improvement was still clinically significant for brain damaged children as shown in Table 25.

3. *Degree of Psychiatric Impairment.* The greatest improvement was found for children with psychiatric impairment of 2 and 3 ratings. Severe psychiatric impairment showed poorer response to medication, although some improvement did result. Complete data are shown in Table 26.

Relationships to Electroencephalogram

There were no statistically significant differences in treatment results for the various EEG types, as shown in Table 27. It should be noted, however, that five children with slow waves showed much less improvement than all the other EEG

TABLE 26

Improvement with Medications According to Degree of
Psychiatric Impairment

Psychiatric Impairment	Methylphenidate		D-amphetamine		Des/Imipramine	
	No. of Patients	Avg. Improvement	No. of Patients	Avg. Improvement	No. of Patients	Avg. Improvement
0	1	0	2	—0.50	0	—
1	14	2.36	12	2.00	7	2.71
2	97	3.31	64	2.94	22	2.86
3	103	2.99	89	2.79	32	3.28
4	47	2.60	35	2.50	9	3.11
5	20	1.90	21	2.19	4	1.25
6	5	1.00	7	0.29	0	—

TABLE 27

Treatment Results for Various EEG Types

	Type of EEG	No. of Patients	Average Improvement for All Drugs
Group I	Normal awake and sleep	174	2.68
	Normal awake only	19	2.11
Group II	6 Hz and 14/6 Hz pos. spikes	174	2.88
	6 Hz pos. spike-waves	41	2.80
	Abnormal fast waves	107	2.73
Group III	Neg. and diphasic spikes	42	3.00
	Neg. spike-waves	33	2.45
Group IV	Slow waves only	5	0.80
	Notched waves	4	2.75
	Hyperventilation abnormality	1	2.00
	Slow waves plus other abnormalities	22	2.91

types. This may be clinically significant inasmuch as slow waves are indicative of depressed cortical functioning (brain damage) rather than cortical irritability; but there are not enough cases to be statistically significant.

The following variables showed no significant correlation with treatment results:

1. IQ
2. Presence or absence of "hard" neurological signs
3. Presence of mental retardation

Dosage and Administration of Medication

In the pharmacotherapy of MBD patients, a number of observations merit reporting. Methylphenidate almost always has to be given more than once a day. Only a few children could be well maintained on a single morning dose. Generally, the daily dosage was divided between morning and noon, often with the morning dose larger since some effects of the morning dose were still present in the afternoon. Many children, however, experienced symptoms in the late afternoon or evening or both requiring an additional dose on returning home from school. This dose was usually smaller than the noon dose. Some children required more frequent dosage since it was clear the medication was losing its effect in those cases after only three or four hours. A few children required a dosage every two hours in order to be maintained in school; otherwise, their behavior or concentration deteriorated to unacceptable levels. The absorption of methylphenidate was in some children quite erratic. Since methylphenidate is absorbed only in the acid medium of the stomach and not in the alkaline medium of the intestine,* it is likely that some of the medication gets washed out of the stomach by food or drink and is thus rendered unabsorbable. It was noted that in a few children given an experimental liquid preparation of meth-

---

* Personal communication, Ciba Pharmaceutical Division.

ylphenidate, the dosage requirement was half of the tablet form. The absorption will thus be better if the dosage is given before meals; however, it should be emphasized that in only a few children was erratic absorption a problem.

Tachyphylaxis was rare with methylphenidate. Only four patients showed an improvement followed by rapid immunity. In one case, a girl with aminoaciduria, who had almost no ability to concentrate, methylphenidate produced amazing concentration which lasted, unfortunately, for just two days. Doubling the dose again improved concentration, again lasting only two days. The third doubling had the same effect but by that time it was clear that this procedure could not be maintained. Two patients showed a good response for several months, then became totally immune to the drug. It was noted that these same two were also helped by des/imipramine, but after several months became totally immune to that drug too. Following this, they were given thioridazine, which again helped for a short time, and was again followed by total immunity. Retrying methylphenidate at this point was completely ineffective. On the other hand, two patients who became immune to methylphenidate after a few months were successfully switched to des/imipramine, became immune to this drug after a few months, but by that time were again responsive to methylphenidate and have been maintained for several years switching back and forth from one drug to the other.

The dosage for methylphenidate ranged from 5 to 140 mg a day, and the frequency of dosage varied from one in the morning to seven doses per day. It should be mentioned that most children are loath to take pills in front of other children and tact is needed in the administration of medication during school hours. Usually the effect of methylphenidate is observed in 20 to 30 minutes, but the full effect may not be visible for several days. Usually when a child omits the medication, a change is noticeable almost immediately, but sometimes it will take two or three days off medication for the changes to be manifest. It is most common, however, for teachers to observe a child for only a few minutes to determine whether or not he has had his medication that day.

D-amphetamine is available in both tablet and time capsule form. The time capsule is especially convenient for once-a-day dosage but lacks flexibility since it is available only in 5, 10, and 15 mg strengths, and some patients do best with 7½ mg or 12½ mg a day. It is possible to combine a time capsule with the tablet form if necessary. D-amphetamine is also available in an elixir for those few patients for whom swallowing a pill or capsule is too much of a struggle. D-amphetamine is effective for longer periods of time than methylphenidate, and it is rare that twice-a-day dosage is inadequate. For tablets, the preferred schedule is morning and noon, again with the larger dose in the morning quite common. Occasionally a patient becomes so wound up as the medication wears off in the evening that he cannot fall asleep, and a small amount at bedtime calms him down. Much more often, however, the effect of a late dosage is to keep the patient awake, and in such cases, most of the daily dosage is concentrated in the morning. The time capsules can usually be used instead of the tablets but problems of absorption are more common with time capsules. Sometimes there is delayed absorption so that parts of the day are inadequately covered, sometimes absorption is incomplete; in such cases the patient can be switched to tablets.

The effects of d-amphetamine are usually apparent, as with methylphenidate, in 20 to 30 minutes, but the full effect may not be present for several days. For this reason, we have usually maintained the medication on weekends even though the only problem may be in school. Otherwise, Monday mornings may be difficult as the dosage may be inadequate for that day.

Des/imipramine is usually administered at bedtime and generally lasts a full 24 hours. The advantages of bedtime dosage are: (1) restless sleep is often improved; (2) enuresis, if present, is maximally helped; (3) any sedative effect of the drug can be ignored—usually the sedative effect wears off after about a week, but by using bedtime instead of morning doses, the resistance of parents who might become upset at some grogginess can be obviated; (4) it eliminates possible embarrassment of children having to take medication in school. Sometimes it is clear that the medication given at bedtime wears off some time during the day. Then the dosage can be switched to the morning, or a twice-a-day schedule may be necessary. Unlike the use of this drug for depression, results are apparent in several hours. If enuresis is present, it may be controlled the first night. It should be noted that des/imipramine was generally more helpful for enuresis than other drugs. In addition, it was definitely the choice for encopresis. Des/imipramine was effective if it was the "accidental type" where the child was "too busy" playing to feel the urge and stained his underpants or eliminated small amounts of feces before he got to the lavatory. Where a child clearly emptied his bowels in his underpants with full knowledge of what he was doing, the drug was, as might be expected, not effective. The dosage ranged from 10 to 350 mg per day and was usually given once a day, but maximally three times a day. (The larger doses were confined to children over twelve.)

Diphenylhydantoin when used was administered three times a day, 5 mg per kilogram total daily dosage unless seizures were present, when four-a-day dosage might be necessary.

Thioridazine was used in dosage from 10 to 300 mg daily administered one to three times during the day. Haloperidol dosage varied between 0.5 to 5 mg daily in two or three dosages. Often an anti-Parkinson drug was needed concomitantly, as dystonias were common side effects.

R-amphetamine was occasionally tried and seemed to work as well as d-amphetamine but not enough data are available to warrant any conclusions. Isocarboxazid, a monoamine oxidase inhibitor, was extremely effective in two cases where it was tried. However, it caused orthostatic hypotension and it was discontinued.* Amitriptyline and nortriptyline were used with several patients with results similar to des/imipramine, but the incidence of side effects was greater. In two retarded patients who could not swallow tablets or capsules, nortriptyline, which is the only tricyclic amine available as a liquid, was used effectively. In several children with grand mal seizures, the addition of d-amphetamine to the anti-convulsants they were taking not only helped behavioral and learning deficiencies but also reduced the incidence of seizures. On the other hand, occasionally methylphenidate increased the incidence of seizures. We saw no effect on seizures from des/imipramine.

As the child gets older, his dosage requirements usually increase until a point is reached, usually in adolescence, where medication no longer has any salutary effect, or, in the case of the stimulants, the former calming effect is replaced by the typical adult reaction of stimulation. It is common in the case of methylphenidate and d-amphetamine for a larger dose to be needed after about six months, with increments every six to nine months. The increment is usually small so that very large doses are rarely necessary. Des/imipramine also requires a larger dose from time to time, but usually not as frequently.

The determination of the end point in treatment is usually made accidentally; that is, the child goes away for a few days without medication or the prescription runs out, and, in contrast to past experience, no change is noted either at home or at school. Sometimes parents see no change, but the teacher at school, which is a more demanding situation, does. In cases of doubt, a "blind" experiment can be tried in which the patient takes no medication or takes placebo for a month or

* Perlstein (1959) and Saunders (1960) have reported benefits from MAO inhibitors.

two and the teachers (the "blind" investigators) are then polled for their observations. If no deterioration in school work or behavior is noted, the medication can then be officially stopped. If deterioration is evident, medication should be continued another year and the trial repeated. Occasionally a child during puberty or abolescence may alter his response to stimulants from the calming to the exciting mode and require the discontinuance of the stimulants—yet he may still have trouble with concentration, perception, memory or behavior. In such a case, switching to des/imipramine is usually effective.

The oldest patient we have had on the stimulants is 21, but a number of patients taking des/imipramine are benefited sufficiently even as young adults to warrant its continuance. The earliest age at which a patient outgrew the need for medication was age 10. The modal age for discontinuance of medication is 16. Children with frank brain damage may require medication for much longer periods of time. Those who benefit from diphenylhydantoin, or one of the phenothiazines, especially may require continuation through adulthood.

Improvement of Behavior

Almost all behavioral improvement could be reduced to improvement in control systems: less restlessness, less distractibility, less impulsiveness, fewer emotional explosions, better motor coordination. In many cases, results were visible within a half hour, but maximum improvement, to some extent, depended on a formation of new habits. As would be expected, the formation of new habits is easier for the younger age group than for the adolescent. A good example of this is our observation of a number of cases who were students at a local private school for children with learning disabilities. In this school, the younger children, including those who had been behavior problems prior to entering the school, require almost no special treatment or guidance; they settle down easily, and while defects in concentration may still be present, they offer no special problems in handling. When they catch up with their grade level and return to a regular classroom, they generally continue to do well. In contrast, the older children in the school from seventh grade up, even when learning well, may be discipline problems, and they may have difficulty adjusting to the regular classroom when they leave the school. Clearly, the influence of long-standing habits is operating here.

There is much written about the position of a "sick" child in the family—his role as the identified patient in what is really a sick family. For the MBD children, we did not find this to be the case. Even when the family was truly sick, the improvement in the patient resulted not in the decompensation of the family but the opposite—the improvement of family life

A good illustration is provided by Case #358 (page 113) — when the child improved, the violence of his father diminished, and the whole family atmosphere improved. In another case, when the patient improved, his brother's teacher wrote on the report card: "Jimmy has been like a different boy since February, very much calmer and more pleasant." The change coincided with the time that Jimmy's *brother* began receiving treatment; the teacher had been totally unaware of what was going on in the family. In only one case did we note that as one child improved, another got worse, and this was a special case of monozygotic twins (Case #583, page 110) in which the "good twin" became resentful when his position was challenged when the "bad twin," under treatment, became as good as he had been. It was common for parents to remark that their children could play peacefully and calmly until their sibling, the MBD child, entered the scene, when bedlam would quickly ensue; one of the more visible benefits of treatment was the diminution in this bedlam-instigating tendency.

It was our impression that treatment results were better in healthy families and worse in disturbed families, as would be expected, but we could not quantify this. Generally patients with MBD need tight external controls to compensate for their deficiency in internal controls, and in disturbed families external controls are often lacking. Not infrequently we noted that a family was not "disturbed" in the usual psychiatric sense, but that parents were easygoing, sentimental, and "tender-minded," totally unable to see themselves in the role of strict and tough-minded parents; in these families, it was noted that the MBD child tended to create difficulties which the parents could not handle; whereas their non-MBD siblings thrived. In truly disturbed families, we frequently saw pre-pubertal MBD children do very well with treatment only to deteriorate as adolescence came and with it greater aggressiveness and testing of controls. Case #1042, page 118, is a good example.

Improvement in Learning

The most immediate improvement is in the area of increased concentration. This allows the child to spend more of his school time in actual learning. Occasionally, it allows him to grasp concepts that he previously could not grasp as in Case #264, page 133. Little is known about the neurophysiology of the learning process itself, but in our cases, we can separate to some extent several types of problems in learning which can be improved with treatment: (1) defects in concentration; (2) defects in perception; (3) defects in language, both receptive and expressive; (4) defects in memory, both storage and retrieval; (5) defects in fine motor coordination.

Impairment in concentration can be seen clearly demonstrated in Case #900, page 121. Figures 3 and 4 are school papers done by a child on medication and figures 5 and 6 are papers done by the same child after medication had been stopped for a week. These school papers are typical of the work done with and without medication.

Sometimes perception is noticeably improved immediately. Visual-motor perception can be illustrated with such tests as the Bender-Gestalt and by drawings, and one sometimes sees dramatic changes over a few days. Figure 7 illustrates how an 8-year-old child, unable to copy a triangle or diamond (normally done by a child when he reaches ages 5 and 7 respectively), is able to do so after being on medication one day. Figures 8, 9, 10 and 11 illustrate the difference in quality of drawing before and after medication. Defects in understanding and expression of language are often noted. Teachers may comment that without medication a child does not seem able to grasp instructions or cannot express what he was able to do just the day before. One of our children, Case #264, was able to gain three years of reading in just a few weeks because he was suddenly able to grasp phonics.

Defects in memory are common. It is frequently noted that a child may, for example, learn a group of words working with his mother in the evening and forget everything by the next morning. Medication frequently helps with memory functions.

Adverse Reactions and Side Effects

Adverse reactions and side effects of the medications were recorded and graded on a scale of 0 to 3. Zero indicates no side effects whatsoever; 1 indicates very mild side effects which do not warrant change in medication; 2 indicates moderate side effects which are not severe enough to warrant discontinuation of medication; 3 indicates severe side effects which warrant immediate discontinuance of medication.

Of 618 patients in which pharmacotherapy was begun, 114 complained of one or more side effects from active medication

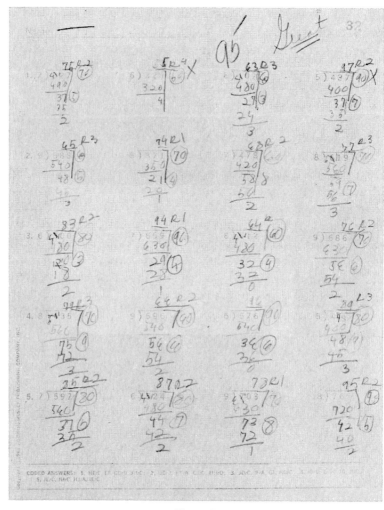

Figure 3.
Case #900. School Paper While Taking D-Amphetamine.

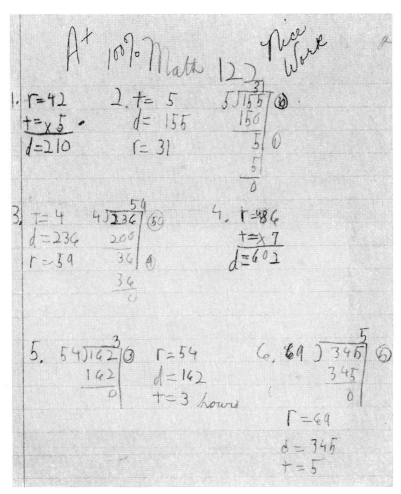

Figure 4.
Case #900. School Paper While Taking D-Amphetamine.

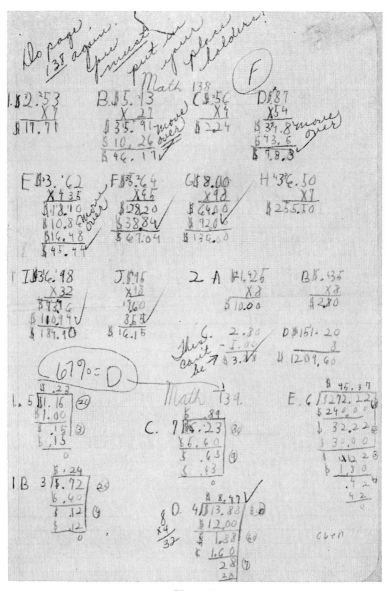

Figure 5.
Case #900. School Paper After Medication Was Omitted For A Week.

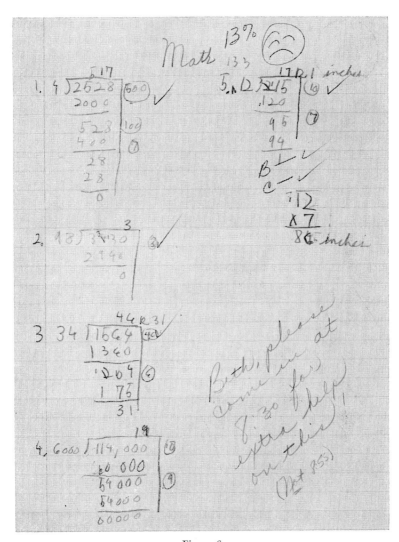

Figure 6.
Case #900. School Paper after Medication Was Omitted for a Week.

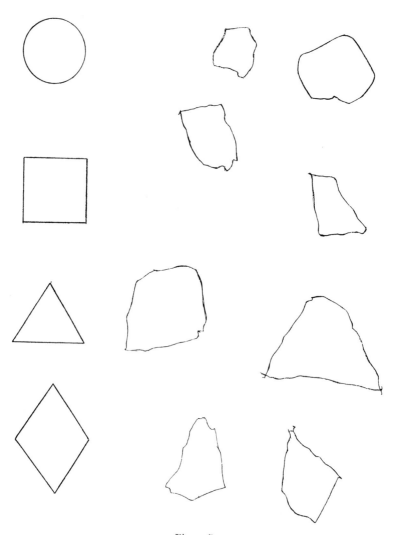

Figure 7
Visual-motor Deficits in 7½-year-old Boy

Middle column done early in morning before medication, right-hand column 1 pm same day after two doses of methylphenidate.

Figure 8.
Case #1006. Draw-A-Person, No Medication.

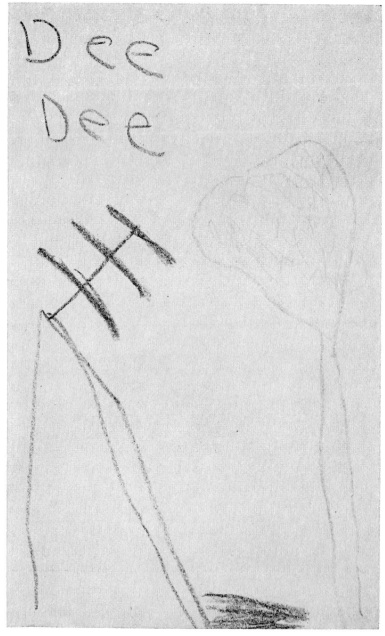

Figure 9.
Case #1006. House and Tree, No Medication.

Figure 10.
Case #1006. Draw-a-Person Done One Month After Figure 8, After Taking Imipramine One Week.

Figure 11

Case #1006. House and Tree Done One Month After Figure 9, After Taking Imipramine One Week.

TABLE 28

Side Effects of Treatment According to Severity

Severity of Side Effects	Number of Side Effects		
	Methylphenidate 377 patients	D-amphetamine 371 patients	Des/Imipramine 149 patients
Grade 1	43 (12%)	47 (13%)	7 (4.7%)
Grade 2	12 (3.2%) ⎱ (4.3%)	11 (3.0%) ⎱ (7.3%)	4 (2.7%) ⎱ (7.4%)
Grade 3	4 (1.1%) ⎰	16 (4.3%) ⎰	7 (4.7%) ⎰
Total Side Effects	59 (16%)	74 (20%)	18 (12%)

and two complained of side effects from placebo. In some cases, there were side effects from two or three medications given the same patient. If very mild side effects are excluded, 38 of the 618 or 6.1% had significant side effects. Table 28 details the side effects noticed from the various medications most commonly used. It should be noted that very mild side effects were considerably less for des/imipramine than for methylphenidate or d-amphetamine, but the more severe side effects were considerably less for methylphenidate than for d-amphetamine or des/imipramine. A detailed list of all side effects recorded, segregated by body system involved, is given in Table 29. From these two tables, it is evident that d-amphetamine has the highest total incidence of side effects, 20%; and des/imipramine the lowest incidence of side effects, 12%. Looking at the incidence of the severe side effects—severe enough to warrant immediate discontinuation of the medication—it is very low, 1.1%, for methylphenidate, while it is slightly over 4% for d-amphetamine and des/imipramine. Thus, for none of these medications is the incidence of severe side effects high by any reasonable standard. For a given patient, a major side effect occurring with one medication suggests that one should try another; particularly between the stimulants and des/imipramine there is very little overlapping

TABLE 29

Detailed List of Side Effects by Type and Grade of Severity

Number of Specific Side Effects*

Side Effects by Type	Methylphenidate 377 Patients			D-amphetamine 371 Patients			Des/Imipramine 149 Patients		
	Gr 1	Gr 2	Gr 3	Gr 1	Gr 2	Gr 3	Gr 1	Gr 2	Gr 3
Psychiatric									
Crabby, touchy, whiny	1	0	0	7	0	0	0	0	0
Delirious	0	0	0	0	0	1	0	0	0
Depression, crying, morbid thoughts	3	1	0	3	0	0	1	0	1
Estrangement	0	0	1	0	0	1	0	0	0
Fearfulness	0	0	0	0	0	0	0	0	1
Hallucinations	0	0	0	0	0	1	0	0	1
Nightmares	2	0	0	0	1	1	0	0	0
Withdrawn	1	0	0	0	0	0	0	0	0
Total number	7	1	1	10	1	4	0	0	3
Percentage	1.9%	0.3%	0.3%	2.7%	0.3%	1.0%	0%	0%	0.8%
Central Nervous System									
Bizarre body movements	1	0	0	0	0	2	0	0	0
Dizziness	2	1	0	0	0	0	0	0	0
Drowsiness	0	1	0	0	0	0	1	0	1
Headache	3	0	0	2	0	1	1	0	1
Insomnia	8	1	1	13	1	2	2	0	0
Jitteriness	0	0	0	1	0	0	0	0	0
Petit mal seizures	0	0	0	0	1	0	0	0	0
Restlessness	1	0	0	0	0	0	0	0	0
Tics	0	2	0	1	1	0	0	0	0
Total number	15	5	1	17	3	5	3	0	2
Percentage	4.0%	1.3%	0.3%	4.6%	0.8%	1.3%	2.0%	0%	1.3%

TABLE 29 (*Continued*)

Number of Specific Side Effects*

Side Effects by Type	Methylphenidate 377 Patients			D-amphetamine 371 Patients			Des/Imipramine 149 Patients		
	Gr 1	Gr 2	Gr 3	Gr 1	Gr 2	Gr 3	Gr 1	Gr 2	Gr 3
Gastrointestinal									
Anorexia	10	3	1	18	5	1	1	1	1
Nausea	4	2	0	2	0	1	2	1	0
Stomachaches	8	0	0	0	1	1	0	0	0
Vomiting	0	0	0	0	0	1	0	0	0
Total number	17	5	1	20	6	4	3	2	1
Percentage	4.6%	1.4%	0.3%	5.4%	1.6%	1.0%	2.0%	1.3%	0.7%
Allergic									
Rash	0	0	1	0	0	2	0	1	1
Percentage	0%	0%	0.3%	0%	0%	0.6%	0%	0.7%	0.7%
Other									
Dilated pupils	1	0	0	0	0	0	1	0	0
Enuresis	1	0	0	0	0	0	1	0	0
Fainting spells	1	0	0	0	0	0	0	0	0
Formication	0	1	0	0	0	0	0	0	0
Glazed eyes	0	0	0	0	0	1	0	0	0
Weakness	1	0	0	0	0	0	0	1	0
Weight loss	0	0	0	1	1	0	0	0	0
Total number	4	1	0	0	1	1	2	1	0
Percentage	1.0%	0.3%	0%	0%	0.3%	0.3%	1.4%	0.7%	0%

* Some patients had more than one side effect.

of side effects. It should be noted that in some cases listed in Tables 28 and 29, more than one side effect was reported per patient. The average number of side effects for each patient reporting any side effect at all was 1.3.

The most prominent side effects are clearly anorexia (reported by 41 patients) and insomnia (reported by 28 patients). D-amphetamine was most commonly implicated for both these symptoms and des/imipramine least.

In two-cases, d-amphetamine had been used successfully and without side effects for about two years, and then rather suddenly side effects developed—in one case severe nausea, and in the other nausea and glazed eyes.

Aside from anorexia, no long-term side effect was noted for any of the medications. When anorexia was mild, it usually disappeared after a few months, or was counteracted with supplemental meals or bedtime snacks. When cyproheptadine was approved for use in anorexia, we began prescribing it before meals, with marked benefit in restoring the appetite. When anorexia was more than mild, medication was reduced or switched to some other kind.

Growth Studies

In studies of the growth patterns of children, Safer and Allen (1973) found that in 29 children who took d-amphetamine for an average of 2.9 years, there was a loss of expected weight of 20 percentile points, and a loss of expected height of 13 percentile points. For 20 patients receiving methylphenidate, there was less of a loss: 6 percentile points in weight and 5 in height. In terms of absolute height and weight gain, those on d-amphetamine gained 2.1 instead of the expected 3.4 kg, and 4.5 instead of the expected 6.0 cm; those on methylphenidate gained 0.5 kg and 1.0 cm less than expected. No loss of growth was experienced when the daily dose was less than 20 mg. Controls who received no medication gained slightly more than expected. They suggested medication be omitted when the child is not in school.

For our patients, we endeavored to assemble as many growth curves as possible for patients who had been taking medication for two or more years. We were able to obtain 61 growth curves altogether, using data taken from school or physicians' records.

For des/imipramine we have 10 growth curves, representing an average duration of 4.3 years on medication; the dosage ranged from 25 to 350 mg daily and averaged 90 mg. From the curves we could find little consistent or significant change in height or weight development during the time the patients were taking medication, with one exception, in which either the growth or the measurement of growth was so erratic that no interpretation could be made.* A typical set of growth curves is shown in Figure 12. There were two cases in which there was a slight loss of expected weight but not of height, and one case in which there was a slight loss of both expected weight and height; in all three cases the expected height and weight were regained by adolescence, while the patients were still taking medication. The set of growth curves for the last-mentioned patient is shown in Figure 13. Three cases showed increases in expected weight.

For d-amphetamine, 3 out of 15 patients showed some loss of expected weight, but only one showed a possible loss of expected height, and this was small, 2 cm at age 12. Patients who have been followed through adolescence seem to have a growth spurt that returns any weight reduction to the expected growth pattern, as shown in Figure 14. In one case, shown in Figure 15, both weight and height growth, after an initial diminution, returned to expected values during adolescence while the patient was still taking the medication. The average dose of the patients taking d-amphetamine for whom

---

* All growth curves were reviewed by a specialist in growth, Sheldon Waldstein, M.D.

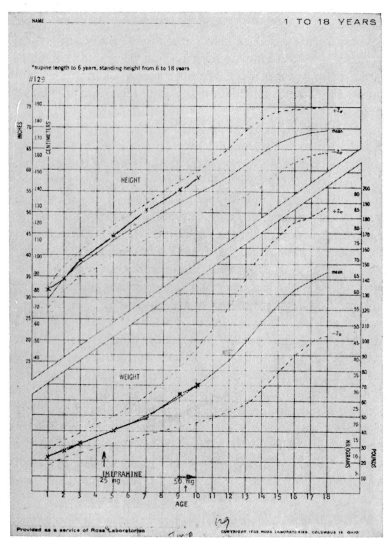

Figure 12.
Growth Curves for Typical Patient Taking Imipramine.

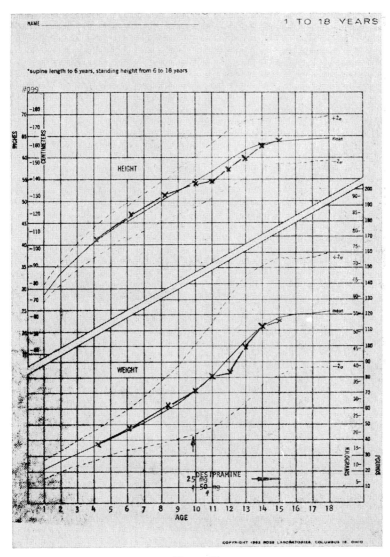

Figure 13.
Growth Curves of Patient Showing Initial Loss of Expected Height and
Weight with Subsequent Recovery of Both While Still Taking Desipramine.

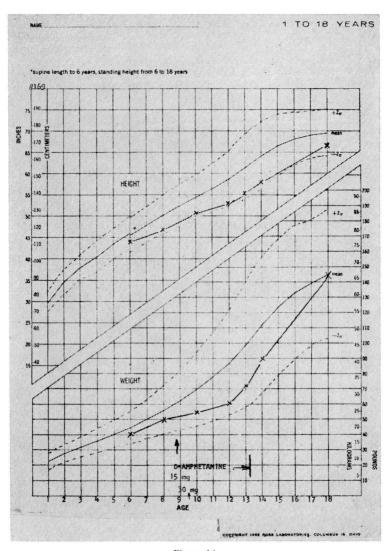

Figure 14
Growth Curves of Patient Taking D-Amphetamine, Showing Initial Loss of
Expected Weight Completely Regained by Adolescence.

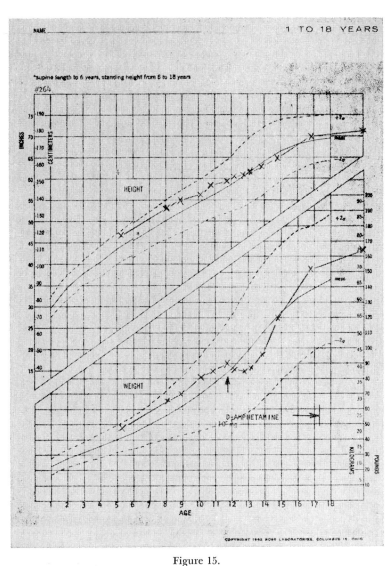

Figure 15.
Growth Curves of Patient Taking D-Amphetamine Showing Initial Loss of
Both Expected Height and Weight Completely Regained by Adolescence.

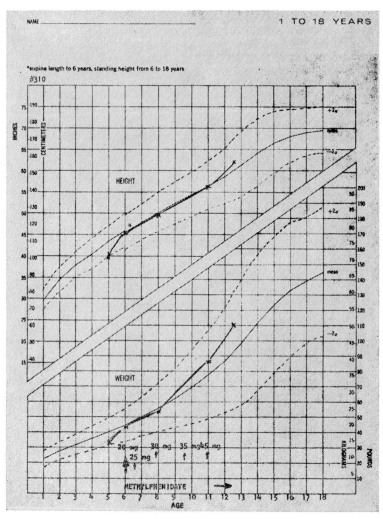

Figure 16.
Typical Growth Curves of Patient Taking Methylphenidate.

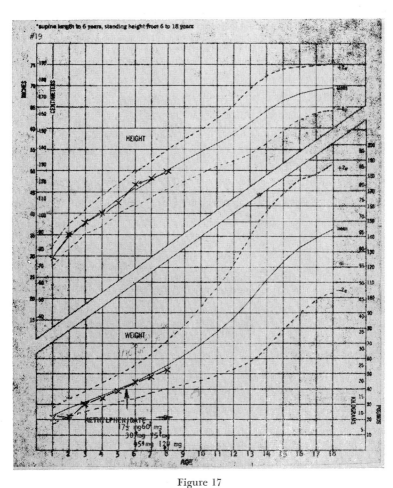

Figure 17
Typical Growth Curves of Patient Taking Methylphenidate. Note High
Dosage.

we have growth curves is 15 mg daily, with a range of 5 to 30 mg; the average duration is 4.9 years.

Since anorexia was the most common side effect of d-amphetamine, it is not surprising that there might be some slowing of weight growth. What is surprising is that some slowing of weight growth was found even where no anorexia was reported. Some parents have remarked, "He eats like a horse but still doesn't gain." Possibly, as Safer (1973) suggests, some unexpected mechanism is at work.

We have 39 growth curves for patients taking methylphenidate. Daily dosages averaged 33 mg, varying between 10 and 120 mg, and the average duration of medication was 4.5 years. Twenty-four patients showed no loss in expected height or weight. Typical curves are shown in Figures 16 and 17. Eight children showed some loss of expected weight but no loss of expected height. Seven showed some losses in both expected weight and expected height; three of these fully regained and one has almost regained their expected height and weight; a representative set of growth curves is shown in Figure 18 (page 109).

One case at age 14½ has not regained his expected height and weight, which are 5 cm (2 inches) and 10 kg below what would have been expected from his growth curve prior to taking methylphenidate. His daily dosage for the most part has been 30 mg. Another case, an obese boy, has shown some weight loss while taking 20 mg daily of methylphenidate, and also some slowing of height development (10 cm less than expected) ; he is only 11½, and it remains to be seen whether in adolescence his expected height will be regained, as happened with so many others. Another obese boy, at age 14, taking 35 mg daily, shows some slowing in height growth (7 cm) . Both these obese boys were at the 95th percentile of height, and even with the slowing of growth are still considerably above average in height at the time of the last measurement. In contrast to the data of Safer, some patients failed to make expected weight growth even on 20 mg a day. Four patients showed greater than expected weight growth, and two showed greater than expected growth in height and weight while taking methylphenidate.

In summary, three of 39 patients taking methylphenidate appear to have sustained some loss of expected height; only one of these is below average in height. None of these has completed adolescence, so that it is still possible they will catch up later. We agree with Safer et al. (1973) that the problems of untreated MBD outweigh any loss of height; yet, we believe it would be prudent to keep height and weight records on all patients taking stimulants so that trends can be detected early. As with d-amphetamine, some loss of expected weight took place without any anorexia reported. When patients show a loss of expected height or weight, steps can be taken to eliminate medication on weekends and during school vacations, supplemental nutrition can be suggested, or cyproheptadine tried.

Quantitatively, our data appear to contradict those of Safer, but the longer time period of observation we have may prove to be crucial, if it should be the case that losses in expected growth are "made up" during adolescence. We have taken several cases of loss of expected height and plotted them as *rate of growth*. These data tend to support the notion of a delay in growth rather than a suppression.

Blood Pressure

We could find no abnormalities in blood pressure from long-term use of these medications.

For children from ages 5 to 10, all blood pressures recorded ranged between 90/60 and 104/80. For children 11 to 18, all systolic pressures recorded ranged between 90 and 120, diastolic between 60 and 80.

Of these children, 24 had been taking methylphenidate from 6 months to $6\frac{1}{2}$ years, with an average of 3.5 years. Nineteen children had been taking d-amphetamine from 7 months to 7 years, with an average of 2.9 years. Eighteen had been taking des/imipramine from 7 months to 5 years, with an average of 2.2 years.

Addiction

We have never seen a child habituated, much less addicted, to any of the medications used. Children tend to resist taking medicines, and even those mature enough to realize their benefit and to take them faithfully would occasionally forget. Most of the time they have to be reminded and occasionally forced to take their medication. Addiction or habituation occurs only when there is a pleasant alteration of consciousness; with these medications, in children, there is none. *We can categorically state that the risk of addiction is zero.*

Personality Changes

Contrary to the report of Stewart (1973), we have seen no "drugged personality" or "undrugged personality" which confuses a child. A child who is overmedicated may have a "personality change;" this is corrected with a correction in dosage. A formerly rambunctious child may, under medication, become so quiet that the change is disturbing to the parents. When one finds a significant change in a child's personality—becoming too quiet, for example—the dosage or medication is not correct for that child and should be changed. For example, sometimes a child who is used to acting out by screaming or throwing temper tantrums may "act in," and under a similar stimulus react by crying or sulking instead of screaming or kicking. This usually is the beginning of increased self-control. But most children—almost all, in fact—have no perception that the medication has any effect on them. If asked about any effect, almost all answer that they cannot tell any difference, regardless of whether parents or teachers find them vastly improved, the same, or worse. In seeing several hundred children through adolescence, we have found no difficulties whatsoever in eventually discontinuing medication.

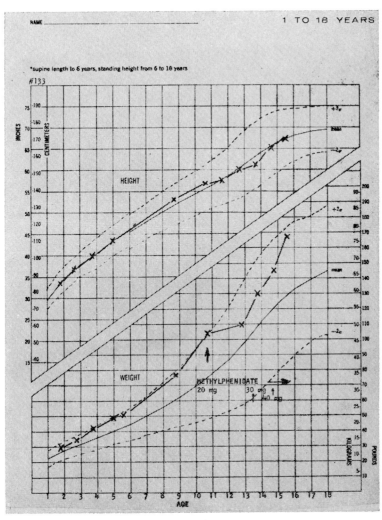

Figure 18.
Growth Curves of Patient Taking Methylphenidate Showing Initial Loss of
Expected Height and Weight Almost Completely Regained by Mid-Adoles-
cence While Still on Medication.

7

Case Studies

Some typical case histories are included in this section. An attempt has been made to give a wide selection of various problems which can be manifestations of MBD.

Case #583—Monozygotic Twins—One with Behavior Disorder, the Other without

Jim and Jon are monozygotic twins, proved by laboratory studies. They were 9 years old when Jim came to our attention because of his behavior in school. Their mother had nine children, but only Jim was a problem. Jon, on the other hand, was a "model child." Both infants appeared normal at birth; however, they were colicky during their first four months. Thereafter Jon developed into a pleasant, appealing baby, who was always good-natured and easy to get along with. On the other hand, Jim, who had been born first and whose delivery had been more difficult, became increasingly fussy and irritable, and would fly into a rage with little provocation. The temper tantrums got worse with age, and had become so severe that he was in danger of being expelled from school. Physical examinations had never revealed any abnormalities.

Both twins had an EEG. Jon's was normal but Jim's revealed numerous left temporal spikes. Jim was given methsuximide, 300 mg each morning. His behavior changed dramatically: his temper tantrums ceased entirely. His school teacher reported he had become a "model child" very much like his twin, and she could not believe it was the same boy. Six months later, the family ran out of methsuximide and for three days he received no medication. His mother immediately noticed a return of the temper tantrums, and the school called home to report the same thing. When methsuximide was resumed, his behavior again improved dramatically.

At age 15 the EEG was repeated on both, with the same findings as before. By age 16 medication was discontinued; there was a slight increase in irritability, but no other change. Both have now completed college and are doing very well.

As an interesting psychological footnote, it was noted that after Jim had improved so greatly with the medication, Jon, who for many years had enjoyed the position of being the "good twin," reacted to Jim's becoming "good" by marked jealousy and resentment, which took several years to dissipate.

Several years later, a younger brother and younger sister were referred for poor concentration in school. Neither was any behavior problem. Both were found to have 14/6 Hz positive spikes on the EEG, and both did well with methylphenidate.

Case #782—Adolescent Girl with Shyness and Auditory Perceptual Defect

This girl was first seen at age 14 with complaints that she was shy, preoccupied, slow in manner and unable to make friends. She had a slight strabismus and her family was very concerned about this. Mother was in an automobile accident during her fifth month of pregnancy with this child. Labor was long and during the first week of her life her eyes were said to "wander to the corners." At age 3, she had measles and the eyes were reported again as "wandering." She walked at age 16 months and began to talk in sentences at age one year. She was enuretic to age 8. Onset of menses was at age 11. Two younger sisters are described as just the opposite of patient, ambitious, aggressive, with lots of friends.

Examination revealed a plain-looking, quiet, shy, passive, compliant, retiring child who seemed unable to commit herself to a course of action, and would take an inordinate amount of time to become involved with some action when the situation demanded it. A WISC was administered revealing a Verbal IQ of 106; Performance IQ, 86. Visual-motor and auditory perceptual channels were defective. An EEG revealed small sharp spikes alternating between the left and right temporal areas.

She was given various medications of which d-amphetamine worked best. She continued to take d-amphetamine, 10 mg time capsule in the morning, for three years at which time it was increased to 15 mg. Aside from loss of appetite, she did extremely well. Her school work improved, the preoccupation disappeared and she became more aggressive socially. She referred to the medication as "hearing pills" because without them she felt she didn't hear properly. Presumably this referred to improvement in auditory perception.

After three years of this treatment, the WISC was repeated revealing a Verbal IQ of 113, an increase of 7 points, and a Performance IQ of 108, an increase of 22 points. She was still rather shy and timid at this time. In addition to the improvement in intellectual functioning, projective tests also indicated moderate improvement. A repeat EEG at age 18 was normal. She entered college, had some difficulty academically but worked very hard at it and did succeed. Her social adjustment gradually improved. A double-blind experiment with placebo capsules looking identical to d-amphetamine capsules was instituted to see whether medication was still helpful, and at this time, she definitely could tell that the active medication was helpful to her. Medication was discontinued at age 21. She completed college, and married at age 23.

Case #358—Severe Behavior Disorder with Chaotic Home Environment

This 6-year-old boy was referred because he was constantly in trouble at school as well as with his neighbors and with his own family. In kindergarten he was observed to have very changeable moods, sometimes becoming extremely wild and violent, punching and poking other children, knocking them down and taking their toys; at other times, daydreaming, rocking back and forth passively. Occasionally, he would have a severe temper-outburst. Since infancy, he had been an overactive, nervous child, and a leader in the family when it came to making trouble. There were one older and two younger brothers, all three of whom eventually became patients for treatment of their hyperactivity; however, of the four children, this child was definitely the most difficult by far. He had a knack of provoking his father, who would then fly into a violent rage himself and beat him quite mercilessly. It would have been natural to have ascribed all his difficulties to the chaotic and punitive environment at home.

An EEG revealed bi-temporal sharp negative spike activity and several bursts of atypical generalized spike-wave seizure activity, as well as atypical parietal activity during sleep. A WISC revealed a Verbal IQ of 91, Performance IQ, 76. On the Wide Range Achievement Test, reading and arithmetic were close to zero. Verbal concepts, visual motor perceptual functioning and impulse control were at an extremely low level.

Methsuximide, 600 mg daily, and d-amphetamine, 15 mg daily, were prescribed. There was considerable improvement, but the school still could not tolerate him in kindergarten, and he was excluded for the last three months of the school year. The following fall he was admitted to a special class for brain dysfunctional children. In this class, he did remarkably well. He learned at an amazing rate and showed no behavioral disturbances whatsoever. Even though the situation at home was poor—the mother worked part-time and the children were unsupervised much of the time—the atmosphere improved considerably as the parents, particularly the father, responded to the child's improvement.

After 8 months in this special class, he was given the WISC again. The Verbal IQ had risen from 91 to 113, and the Performance IQ from 76 to 107. The Wide Range Achievement Test also had shown remarkable improvement over the year previously: reading from 0 to 4.1, spelling from 0 to 3.4, and arithmetic from 0 to 2.9. The following fall he was placed in a regular class and since that time has done well academically.

EEG data are available on the entire family. Father's and mother's were both negative. Two brothers had EEG's with 14/6 Hz positive spikes. One brother's EEG was negative. The patient himself had a repeat EEG eight years after the first and this revealed only 14/6 Hz positive spikes. (All the brothers eventually became patients because of hyperactivity, and all improved with medication.)

At age 7 the methsuximide was discontinued with no apparent effect, but when the d-amphetamine was omitted for a few days, he became hyperactive and hyperaggressive. At age 11 he began to have problems in school. These were not behavioral problems, but fears of failing and chronic depression. Occasionally he would lash out at one of the family members but not in school. At this point, imipramine, 50 mg at bedtime, was added, and this seemed to be of considerable benefit. Around this time, his father suddenly died and his mother began to work full-time. The whole family appeared to be out of control. His grades fell from good to average, but behaviorally he maintained himself at a good level. Mother is currently receiving treatment to help handle the family problems.

Cases #1011 and 1012—Monozygotic Twins, Hyperactivity and Learning Problems

John and Steve were 7 when they were first seen because of problems in school. Because of their similarities and differences, they will be described in adjoining columns.

JOHN:

STEVE

Chief complaints:
Lack of comprehension, inability to follow a discussion or contribute to it. In a daze most of the time. Aggressive and hyperactive. Speech defect. Enuresis.

Hyperactive, aggressive, temper. Classroom work was not good, but better than John's. More active than John, less distractible.

Past History:
Pregnancy and delivery uncomplicated. Early development within normal limits. Rectal polyps removed at age 6.

Early development within normal limits. Age 4, severe chicken pox. Mild asthma. Nightmares.

Psychological Tests at Age 6½:
WISC: Verbal IQ, 84
     Performance IQ, 103
Wide Range Achievement Tests:
    Reading: 4 Percentile
    Spelling: 18 Percentile
    Arithmetic: 4 Percentile

WISC: Verbal IQ, 95
     Performance IQ, 93
Wide Range Achievement Tests:
    Reading: 4 Percentile
    Spelling: 30 Percentile
    Arithmetic: 8 Percentile

Major Weaknesses on WISC:
    Auditory recall
    Arithmetic memory

Synthesis of parts into whole. Ability to comprehend total situation

Clinical Examination:
Much more speech defect. Left handed. Not "with it," vague

Only mild speech defect. More fidgety. Right handed. Sharper mentally.

Drawings (done separately):
Drew a house with a fence, flowers, clouds, and sun

Almost identical to John's except chimney on left side of house, John's on right side. Very similar colors. Somewhat neater

JOHN:

STEVE:

EEG:
14/6 Hz positive spikes both hemi-spheres

14/6 Hz positive spikes both hemi-spheres, lower voltage and less in amount than John's EEG.

Treatment:
Of various medications, did best with methylphenidate. Considerably improved at school, but not as much as Steve. Enuresis better but still present. Desipramine prescribed for enuresis, but no benefit, so discontinued. Some decrease of appetite, some insomnia. Thioridazine, 10 mg at bedtime, prescribed for this.

Did best also on methylphenidate. Improvement in school greater than John's. Teacher says, "Steve is like a different person. Still triggers easily, loses temper."

Course:
Age 7½: Enrolled in special school for MBD children.

Enrolled in special school for MBD children; different class from John.

Methylphenidate increased because of hyperactivity, from 20 to 30 mg daily. Thioridazine increased from 10 to 30 mg.

Methylphenidate increased because of hyperactivity but did not help. Thioridazine prescribed, dose gradually increased to 50 mg daily.

Age 8: Doing well in school, but at times loud. Gets speech therapy.

Doing very well in school.

Age 8 yrs. 6 mos.: Behavior peculiar: stares off into space, faints. Diagnosis of seizure made, diphenylhydantoin prescribed, 50 mg, t.i.d.

Age 8 yrs. 7 mos.: Much better, behavior back to usual, learning well —for first time learning better than Steve.

Age 8 yrs. 11 mos.: Recurrence of seizures. Violent outbursts. Diphenylhydantoin increased but produced toxicity without eliminating seizures. EEG normal. Hospitalized, echoencephalogram, brain scan and neurologic examination negative. EEG now shows disorganization, slowing and paroxysmal sharp waves.

JOHN:

Ethosuximide prescribed with abolition of seizures and outbursts. Discharged with ethosuximide, diphenylhydantoin, imipramine and thioridazine.

Age 10: Generally has done well. Making good progress in school. Taking ethosuximide, 250 mg, once daily; thioridazine, 50 mg, b.i.d.; diphenydantoin, 50 mg, b.i.d.; and imipramine, 25 mg, b.i.d.

Age 10½: Psychological tests given. WISC:

    Verbal IQ, 82
    Performance IQ, 87

Age 11½: Returned to regular school. Doing quite well.

Age 12: Doing very well. Learning more effectively than Steve.

STEVE:

Fine in school. Loud and bossy at times at home. Still has frequent nightmares. Continues on methylphenidate, now 50 mg daily, and thioridazine, now 100 mg daily.

WISC:

    Verbal IQ, 96
    Performance IQ, 93
Back at a regular school.

Past year at regular school very bad. Became quite upset, fearful, lost confidence. Returned to special school for MBD children.

Much better back in special school, but still tremendous loss of confidence, much anxiety.

When the twins were about 10, an older sister was examined because of hyperactivity and slow learning. She improved considerably with methylphenidate. A short time later, a younger brother was brought in for the same problem. He too improved with methylphenidate.

Some time later, the children's mother requested help for herself. She complained of being totally disorganized in the morning, and unable to get going for several hours. She described the feeling as "achy all over" as though her functioning were paralyzed. When given 50 mg of imipramine at bedtime, she reported an instantaneous response: she felt clear-headed and ready to go when she awoke. Her husband confirmed this response.

Case #1042—Behavior Problem with Temporary
Improvement but Ultimate Downhill Course

Timmy was 11 when he was referred to the Mental Health Center because of behavior problems both at home and at school. He did not accept discipline, would lie and steal and have temper tantrums. He got into frequent fights with his brother, Roger, who a little later also became a patient. Early development apparently was normal, but when he was 2½ years old he fell out of a car and fractured his skull. At age 3, he fell down the stairs twice; at age 9, he fell out of a tree and broke his femur. When he was 6, his father, to whom he was deeply attached, died, and since that time, he seemed to be constantly on the search for a father figure. When he was 8, his mother remarried but his stepfather drank and there were frequent quarrels and home was not happy. At one time during the interview he said, "Dad could be the best dad in the world if he only wanted to." During the interview, he was teary-eyed, tried very hard to control his feelings. He seemed to have a great need to communicate to an older man, and he opened up quite readily. He stated that he gets angry very easily, and although he tries to control himself, he doesn't succeed. He doesn't know why, but he usually ends up fighting.

To the question about what he would wish for if he were granted three magic wishes, he responded, (1) to be smarter in school; (2) to mind his mother and father; (3) not to steal or lie. If he had to be an animal, he would be an ant, "because they can always find cracks where to hide." Then he said, "On second thought, an ant gets into too many fights—I would rather be a squirrel so I can climb trees and see the beautiful world and keep out of danger.

Parents seemed to show very little empathy or understanding for Timmy. They appeared self-centered, angry, preoccupied with their own problems. Neither of them mentioned the alcoholism that seemed to be such an important factor.

An EEG revealed in wake several bursts of 6 Hz positive spike-waves, and in sleep a bi-frontal focus of 20-25 Hz fast activity, in addition to a right temporal focus of 14/6 Hz positive spike activity. A WISC revealed a Verbal IQ of 75; Performance IQ, 82. Thinking was very concrete. He was tried on a number of medications and seemed to do best on d-amphetamine, 15 mg time capsule each morning. His grades improved very slightly, but his conduct in school was very much better and his conduct at home was somewhat better. However, within a few months, he was in difficulty again with fighting and with shoplifting. He said he was not taking his medication, but his mother said he was. He was given a scholarship for a camp that summer and did quite well except for one day when he lost his temper and broke a mirror. He said that day he had not had his medicine for some reason. After the camp experience, he improved considerably and frequently verbalized a determination to make things better for himself. He continued to improve throughout the school year, had a good experience at camp the following summer, but that fall, he and his brother Roger began to get into difficulties more and more frequently. When seen, he seemed extremely upset about all the problems he had. He seemed to actually have been following his younger brother, who was somewhat brighter than he was, in getting into trouble.

By age 14, the troubles began to be quite serious. He stole some money from school by prying open a safe. After that, it was one offense after the other, for which Timmy was put on probation most of the time. However, all of the offenses were against property; none was ever against persons, Timmy was always with another child whom he seemed to follow.

When last seen at age 21, he related he had been off medication since he was 14 years old. He had just gotten divorced from a girl whom he married because she was pregnant. Again he vowed his determination to make things go well for himself, but within a month he was in prison for burglary.

His brother, Roger, aside from being somewhat brighter, was very much like Timmy. His EEG at age 11 showed generalized multiple spiking suggestive of a grand mal component during wake. In sleep, there were intermittent, small, sharp negative spike seizure activity, and additionally fast activity in the bi-frontal areas. He has been in more difficulty than Timmy and has spent more time in prison, where he is currently confined.

Case #765—Hypersensitivity

This 8-year-old girl's mother was undergoing psychotherapy for depression. One of the factors in her depression appeared to be difficult relations with her husband, and one of the main difficulties she complained about was that her husband was very short with Karine, her 8-year-old daughter. He in turn complained that he could not talk to Karine without her crying and whining. For example, at the dinner table if he were to make some criticism of her table manners, she would immediately burst into tears, and this behavior infuriated him. Mother acknowledged that Karine was hypersensitive but basically was a sweet and delightful child. Because of the interweaving of these problems, Karine was brought in to be seen also. In the interview, she appeared a very pretty, sweet girl who seemed to have no problems that could be detected.

An EEG, however, was abnormal, revealing 6 Hz positive spike-waves. On the basis of the EEG findings, she was given placebo and d-amphetamine, 5 mg time capsules in a double-blind experiment. On placebo, there was no change; on active medication, there was a remarkable improvement in her emotional control. The whining and bursting into tears ceased entirely. Her school teacher, who knew nothing of what was taking place, spontaneously remarked on the next report card that Karine seemed to participate much more in class and to be a happier child. She was also getting better grades, A's instead of B's. She continued to take the same medication for two years at which time the family moved away from the area.

Case #900—Underachiever with No Behavior Problems

This 9-year-old girl had no difficulties outside of school. However, in school, she showed little patience, rushed through her work and was quite disorganized. Mother considered her distractible, restless, lazy in school and fidgety. She was about a year behind in her school work, although her IQ (Otis Lennon) was 107.

On examination, she was rather shy but cute, outgoing, and overly grown-up in some ways. She was quite aware of her underachievement and worried a lot about her school work. Her "three wishes" were (1) to be good in school; (2) to be happily married and have healthy children; and (3) to be the prettiest girl in the world. There were no neurologic findings, no visual motor deficits, but considerably distractibility. An EEG was normal.

Of various medications, she did best on d-amphetamine, at first 10 mg, and after two years 12½ mg daily. Her writing became better; she began to enjoy mathematics (her most difficult subject), but she still needed outside help to organize her work. By the following year, her grades were much improved. When medication was omitted for a period due to mother's not supervising this adequately, her school work deteriorated remarkably. Figures 5 and 6 (pages 88, 89) show typical samples of her work without medication and Figures 3 and 4 (pages 86, 87) her work when she was back on medication. There was some loss of appetite from the d-amphetamine. This was counteracted by the use of cyproheptadine, 4 mg before meals, and by bedtime snacks and milk shakes.

A younger brother was found to have similar symptoms and is currently on medication.

*Case #11—Underachievement in School with Some
Behavior Problems*

Jeff was 10 years old when first seen. He was failing fifth
grade and was also a discipline problem in school. He was
less of a problem at home, but even there he would not do as
he was told; his parents would have to keep after him. At
school, church, during family excursions or visits to friends,
he was described as "up and down" all the time. He did not
pay attention to his tasks.

Past history was uneventful. He was a breech delivery, but
this was uncomplicated. At age 15 months, he had a "high"
fever for several days. At age 9½, he had a tonsillectomy, but
otherwise his health had been excellent.

Psychological testing revealed on the WISC a Verbal IQ of
110 and Performance IQ of 121, yet his achievement tests were
below grade average. A report from school stated, "He is not
performing up to his capabilities; he is also very aggressive
with his peers. According to his teachers, his schoolwork is
presently below his ability. He is sloppy and disorganized.
Jeff rarely finishes his work. He is hasty in word and deed.
He talks incessantly and is often rude, often involved in
fights."

On neuropsychiatric examination, he was outgoing, aggressive, friendly, a bit grandiose. His "three wishes" were
(1) money; (2) a big house and swimming pool; and (3)
three more wishes. He tended to rush through tasks; otherwise nothing significant was noted. An EEG revealed 14/6 Hz
positive spikes. Jeff was given a trial of placebo, d-amphetamine, methylphenidate and desipramine. On placebo, he was
described as "terrible." On d-amphetamine, he got his words
mixed up and was excessively clinging. On methylphenidate,
he was much improved except for excessive talking. On desipramine, he was "best so far"; he slept better, was more cheer-
ful in the morning. After a month on desipramine, 25 mg at

bedtime, the teacher reported: "Over all, his academic work has improved in almost all areas. He is less hyperactive and can concentrate for longer periods of time. He participates orally without showing off as he used to. He is less aggressive and argumentative with his peers and with me. He wants to do better." Two months later, because of symptoms recurring in the evenings, the dose was increased by a half tablet given at lunchtime. Achievement tests given at this time showed an average of one year above grade level in contrast to a year below grade level several months prior. By the following year, his grades were better but still lower than his teacher thought he was capable of. His mother currently describes him as expressing more interest in his work, developing friendships and real rapport with other children and possessing much more emotional self-control.

Case #615—Restlessness

This 5-year-old boy is one of six children; two other brothers have also been seen for similar problems, though not as severe. He was referred by the school, but both father and mother were acutely aware that he had problems at home too. He was restless, could not be still a minute, could not keep his interest on things and lost track of ideas very quickly. He was a bright child and did well in school. His father described him as "not naughty, just restless." Yet, he had gotten into more trouble than any of the other children. He was "a daredevil type," breaking his leg before he was a year old. Pregnancy, birth, early development were all within normal limits.

On examination, this youngster appeared very bright with an excellent vocabulary and a great deal of self-confidence. He seemed somewhat hypomanic in manner; at times he got stubborn and pouty quite easily. His attention span was definitely short. Despite his appearance of brightness, on the psychological testing his IQ was barely within the average range.

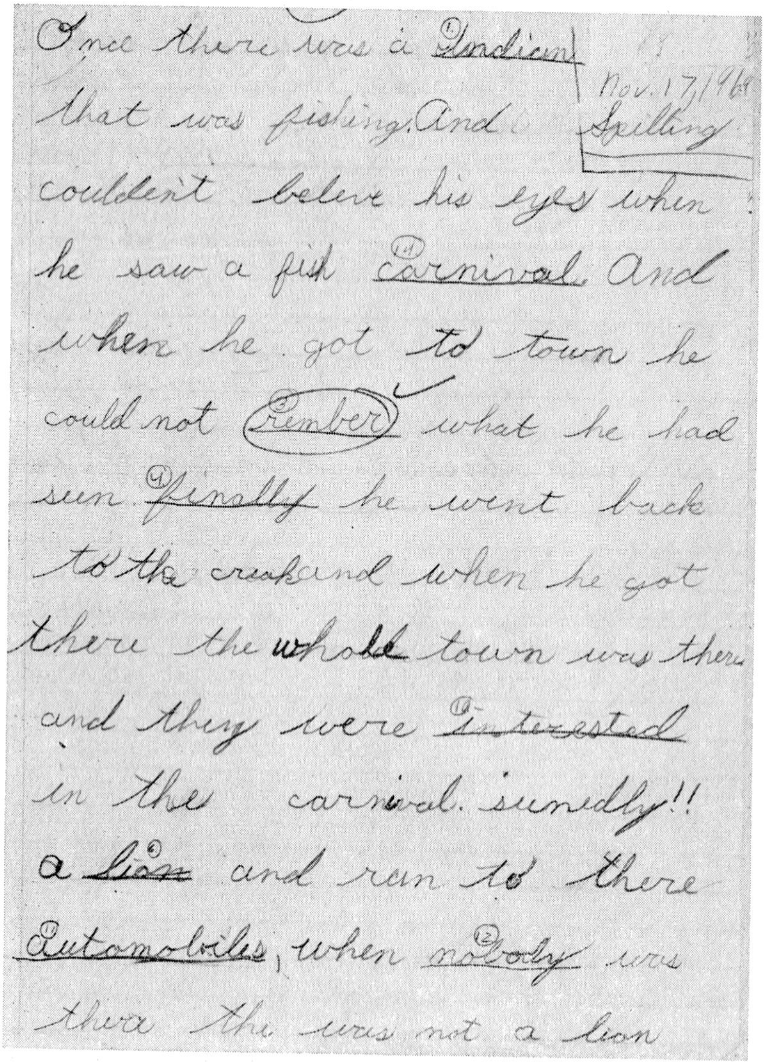

Once there was a Indian
that was fishing. And
couldent beleve his eyes when
he saw a fish Carnival. And
when he got to town he
could not rember what he had
sun finally he went back
to the creak and when he got
there the whole town was there
and they were Interested
in the carnival. suredly!!
a lion and run to there
Automobiles, when nobody was
thea the was not a lion

Nov. 17, 196?
Spelling

Figure 19.
Case #615. School Paper While Taking D-Amphetamine.

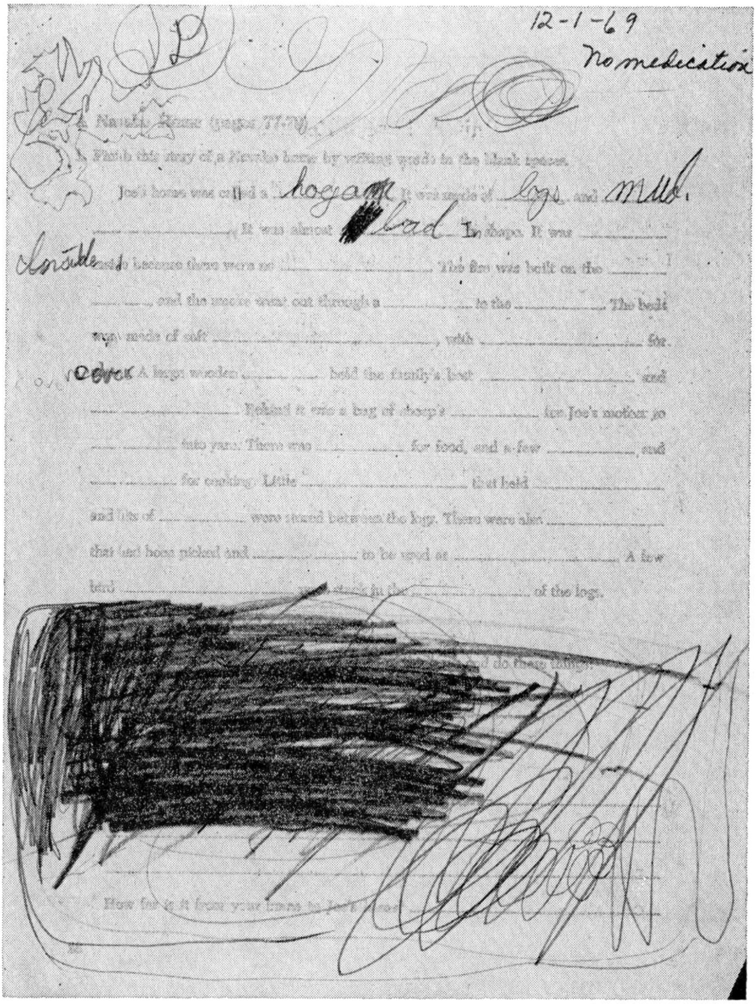

Figure 20.
Case #615. School Paper While Off Medication.

Of various medications tried, d-amphetamine was clearly the best, and has been continued for five years. His schoolwork greatly improved, and he was much easier to handle; however, the poutiness and negativism persisted. For periods of time, he was off medication due to some misunderstanding. Figures 19 and 20 show some of his schoolwork while taking medication and while omitting medication. Each figure is a sample of a stack of papers, all of which were quite similar: that is, on medication, neat, orderly, with good grades; off medication, extremely sloppy with poor grades.

Until age 12, he continued to do quite well in school, but at age 13, his schoolwork dropped off considerably, and his behavior became worse. The family was now in financial difficulties. Part of the problem may have been the irregular taking of medication; part of the problem may have been due to other factors, since the other children in the family were also deteriorating in their schoolwork and behavior.

Cases #442 and 443—Monozygotic Twins, Behavior and Learning Problems

Mark and Michael were first seen at age 10. Of seven children, only the twins had any problems. Mark was rebellious, impulsive and immature; Michael was impulsive and anxious. Both were active babies; both were slow to talk and even at age 5 it was difficult to understand them. Mark overcame his speech problem, but Michael, at age 10, still had immature speech. Both children would rock and roll their heads while going to sleep. Both were toilet-trained rather late, age 3½. In the playroom, Michael was considerably more impulsive than Mark, showed considerably more anxiety and was quite unsure of himself, as well as somewhat bizarre. He seemed clumsy, had visual-motor defects, and a mild thought disorder. Mark was much more self-possessed and showed no evidence of any thought disorder. As an example of their differences, one could quote their response to the question of what they would do if they could have "three magic wishes." Michael's wishes were (1) to be a millionaire; (2) to have faith, hope and love; and (3) to turn into an Oscar Mayer wiener. Mark wished for (1) a chemistry laboratory; (2) to have lots of money so he could buy a stadium and have his own sports program; (3) to have a new bike.

Both had normal EEG's. When tried out on medication, Michael did better on imipramine than on any other; Mark did best on methylphenidate. Over the years, Mark did very well: he was a happy-go-lucky child, a bit scatterbrained, but generally a pleasant child who has worked up to his capacity in school. Michael has not worked up to capacity. He is disorganized and needs more supervision, is more rebellious against doing his assignments both in school and at home. Both have been followed for six years and are still taking medication at age 16.

Case #636—Adolescent with Autism and Isolation

This boy was referred at age 14 because of being withdrawn and overly quiet, not mixing with other children and not achieving in school. He was often teased and rejected by his peers, and in the last few years, he seemed to have substituted railroads for his peer companionship. He spent a great deal of time along the railroad tracks and in the station, memorized all the railroad time tables, and knew every detail about railroads. He was a tall boy but very awkward and clumsy, very poor at athletics. He became angry easily and argued excessively. He was always in a hurry, went through his schoolwork too fast, ran rather than walked; children made fun of him because of his obsession with trains.

Birth was very difficult, but he breathed normally. Early development was uneventful. When he went to school, his handwriting was very poor, but his reading was always good. There was mixed dominance and it took him a long time to settle down to using one hand consistently; he still uses his left hand for certain functions and his right hand for others. When he appeared for the interview, he was bizarrely dressed; his manner was odd; he talked like an old man. He was coherent but not always relevant. His personality was cold but not hostile.

Psychological testing revealed a child who was bright but showed poor reality testing, lack of awareness of community standards, bizarreness of thought and barrenness of affect. An EEG showed abnormal fast waves. With some skepticism, he was given a trial of medication, with very favorable response to d-amphetamine, 15 mg time capsule. He was reported to be much more cooperative at home and easier to get along with at school. He seemed more alert; his appetite was better; he was less inclined to argue. Six months later, on examination, he seemed much less autistic. This time he spoke with enthusiasm about his music. He apparently was doing very well with his musical instrument. He still showed enthusiasm for railroads, but this had a different quality; it seemed much less autistic and more in the nature of a hobby. His goals were much more realistic: he wanted to go to college and then teach music. His mother reported that he still got teased about his interest in railroads, but instead of getting sucked in, he was able to joke about it and had considerably better relationships with his peers. A year later, there was no longer any evidence of autism and he seemed to have forgotten all about railroads. His interest in music had increased. He had been offered a number of scholarships, his grades were much improved, and he was planning to go to college. The last interview was at age 20. He seemed somewhat tense, but otherwise completely appropriate. He was very proud of his accomplishments, which indeed had been considerable in the field of music. A repeat EEG was normal. Medication was discontinued at this point, and a follow-up letter from his mother a year later indicated no change when he stopped the medication. He has had considerable local publicity as a promising young instrumentalist.

Case #1000—Hyperactivity

Jimmy was 7 when referred by the school psychologist because of being hyperactive, bothering other children, lying down on the floor, teasing, pushing, pinching, or doing anything he felt like. He also hummed and sang much of the time. His mother reported that he talked in his sleep all night long and has also walked in his sleep. A younger sister was reported as getting along very well. Past history was uneventful except for a fever of 105° for two days at age 4. However, he was described as not having been any different after the fever, and most of the symptoms of hyperactivity had been present since he was 2 or 2½ years old.

On examination, Jimmy was a nice-looking boy with a rather sluggish manner and some speech defect, with poor articulation of the letter "r." He seemed bright and imaginative and his drawings reflected this. When asked what animal he would choose to be if he had to be an animal, he said he would be a ground hog because nobody could dig and get at him. Although his drawings were imaginative, they were done rather sloppily. Bender-Gestalt figures were copied quite well, but he had difficulty spelling his name, writing it "Jamse" several times. He realized that he had trouble in school and couldn't sit still, but he felt this was because the other children were picking on him and accusing him of things that he didn't do.

The EEG revealed 14/6 Hz positive spiking. He was tried on a number of medications. On both d-amphetamine and methylphenidate he was reported to be less hyperactive and much more settled at school, and to participate more with the rest of the class. He was then given d-amphetamine, 12½ mg each morning. For about six months he did very well, but then his behavior began to regress. The dosage was increased, but this resulted in nausea and so it was reduced again. Within a few months, Jimmy's behavior at school had regressed to where it was originally. He was then switched to methylphenidate, 7½ mg morning and lunchtime. The following report came from the teacher after a month on this medication. "Jimmy has been a different boy since starting the last medication. He has completed work every day for me and does this quietly and seriously. His behavior is much improved. In fact, I didn't realize he could do so well. Of course, some days he has some trouble, talking or moving around in the hall while waiting for me, but what boy doesn't. He volunteers in discussion groups and nearly always knows the answers. It is a joy to see such reaction from him. He shows an increased interest in reading and in extra reading and in library books. The only change in his schedule that has been made is that he has stayed this week in my reading group rather than going to another room. His work in reading group has also improved but not as consistently. Last week he mentioned a preference for staying in my room. After talking to Mr. McCabe, we decided to try this and Jimmy seems happy. He says he likes it better. Perhaps he isn't quite ready for so much change. He probably feels somewhat more secure in this situation. Jimmy is a delightful student and shows much potential and ability right now. I hope it continues this way. He has been more restless today, possibly because he knows he is taking another letter home."

Case #1006—Learning Problems

This 7-year-old girl was referred from school because of learning problems. She had a short attention span, but no behavioral difficulties. She was currently in the first grade in a special developmental first grade class. On the Wechsler Pre-School and Primary Scale of Intelligence, she achieved a Verbal IQ of 89, a Performance IQ of 74. On examination,

she appeared as a very friendly, pleasant, nice-looking girl
with a marked speech defect and many language defects, such
as "him does work in a store." Her drawings were done very
poorly with difficulties in angulation and general poor motor
control. She could not draw a diamond at all and other
simple figures were done poorly. Her gross motor coordination, however, was only slightly below her age level. Her
Draw-a-Person is shown in Figure 8, (p. 91) and her drawing
of a house and a tree in Figure 9. (p. 92) Each drawing was
done only with one color.

There were four other children in the family, and an older
brother was very much as this patient was upon examination
when he started school. The home was somewhat disorganized, but both parents seemed very interested in the problems of the children. Four of the children were only a year
apart, which created difficulties for the mother.

Past history was uneventful except for enuresis occasionally
when she was upset. An EEG showed abnormal fast waves
throughout the record.

Various medications were tried of which imipramine seemed
best. Drawings of a house, tree and person taken one month
after the previous drawings but with imipramine, 20 mg a
day, are shown in Figures 10 (p. 93) and 11 (p. 94). In these
figures there was a great deal of color used as well as a great
deal of time spent giving attention to details. She has been
followed for three years now with the imipramine gradually
being increased, with the current dosage 50 mg a day. Her
schoolwork improved considerably but was still very limited
in its quality. As she grew older, she seemed to withdraw
more. At times she would become overaggressive and at times
negativistic. She was given speech therapy, and her speech
showed gradual improvement. Her language skills increased
considerably, but even at age 10, she had problems with
plurals, tenses and sentence order. From time to time, her
concentration would diminish and there would be increased

random activity. It was at these times that the medication was increased somewhat, with rapid improvement.

Case #626—Immaturity and Daydreaming

Yvonne was six when brought to the Mental Health Center because of immature behavior at home and in kindergarten. She was an only child. Her parents had been divorced a year earlier. The father had a poor work history, drank excessively, and constantly was in conflict with the mother about disciplining Yvonne. In general, he wanted the child to get her own way while the mother wanted her to accept some authority and do things the way her mother thought was correct. The only matter in which father was strict was in regard to table manners. There was constant quarreling between the parents until the divorce.

Yvonne was slow in development in some respects. She did not stand until age 12 months, did not walk until 18 months of age. Other developmental milestones were within normal limits.

On examination, she appeared a small, frail girl, sitting very close to her mother, but leaving her readily when asked to do so. She was quite shy. Her speech was rather infantile; her behavior was quite immature. She seemed overly dependent and helpless for a child her age. Her intellectual level was judged to be low, and subsequent psychological testing did reveal an IQ of 80.

It would have been very simple to have seen this child's immaturity as solely the product of being constantly given into by her father and of having been able to play one parent off against the other. However, the EEG was very abnormal. There were frequent negative spikes occurring in all areas independently, as well as atypical multiple spike and wave discharges in the frontal parietal area and larval grand mal seizure discharges. All forms of seizure activity increased during drowsiness and sleep, with 15 to 18 Hz activity additionally present during drowsiness and light sleep. A number of medications were prescribed. She did best on a combination of methsuximide 150 mg and diphenylhydantoin 25 mg four times a day, and d-amphetamine 5 mg time capsule each morning. By this time she was in first grade; her immature behavior and daydreaming were almost completely gone, but academically, as might be expected from her IQ level, she had considerable difficulty. By fourth grade her behavior continued to improve but academically she was not keeping up and she was transferred to a class for retarded children.

Case #264—Dyslexia, Passivity, Discouragement, with Excellent Response to Medication

Sam, age 11, was referred by his tutor because of learning difficulties. He had had difficulties with speech from the time he learned to talk, and had had many years of speech therapy, with some success. However, his reading had always lagged. He appeared to have a poor concept of phonics, remembering words by rote but not by context. His talk and general behavior tended to be immature, but he was not a troublemaker in school or at home. He was retiring and had few friends. He was passed in school despite his reading problem, and was now in sixth grade but reading at third grade level. His teachers often became upset with him and scolded him frequently, apparently because they thought he could do much better than he did, since he could succeed at non-verbal work. He had begun private tutoring a year ago with gradual improvement in reading from first-grade level to third.

Psychological testing revealed an immature boy filled with passive resignation. The major problem, however, was considered to be an organic language disturbance. The Verbal IQ on the WISC was 80; in contrast, the Performance IQ was 96. The EEG was abnormal, revealing 14/6 Hz positive spike seizure activity.

Sam was given d-amphetamine 10 mg each morning, and acetazolamide 125 mg twice a day. The tutor noticed an immediate change. He could concentrate better, was less tense, and on the first day of his medication he read four pages in his third-grade reader almost perfectly—a marked improvement for him. Mother noted he was more agreeable. In a few weeks his reading level climbed from third grade to sixth grade. He was happy at school and home, and began to lose his shyness and withdrawal. His tutor remarked, "It's unbelievable."

He continued to get extra tutoring in reading throughout junior and senior high school, and while he never read entirely up to grade level he was successful in his schoolwork. He always was able to do well in shop courses, as might be expected from his WISC scores. He completed high school, medication being discontinued in his senior year, and is now, at age 22, an apprentice electrician. He was able to successfully complete a college course in algebra which was necessary for his apprenticeship. Socially, he appears to have good relations with peers and older adults.

Case #228—Brain Damage with Aphasia; No Response to Medication; Subtle Seizures Developing Later Helped by Diphenylhydantoin

This boy was almost 4 years old when first seen. His mother had been in treatment for depression and had expressed concern about his possibly being retarded. His mother had two other children and during all pregnancies, she had developed hypertension and albuminuria. For this boy birth was quite difficult. The cord was wound around his neck several times; he was quite blue when he was born, and he had a difficult time breathing. He was slow in developing: he walked at age 18 months and at age 3 years, 10 months, was able to put only two words together. Toilet training was accomplished easily, however, by age 2.

When seen by the psychologist at age 4, it was impossible to administer formal testing. The EEG revealed a left temporal negative spike discharge focus. Many medications were tried at this time in an effort to improve his extreme restlessness; all seemed to make him worse. At age 5½ he was seen again by a psychologist who administered a Stanford-Binet and obtained an IQ of 61. The impression was that this was definitely a retarded child. Six months later the Performance half of the WISC was administered and this resulted in an IQ of 94, which led to the consideration that patient was not retarded but was aphasic. The re-test of the WISC at age 6½ revealed a Verbal IQ of 55 and a Performance IQ of 101 and the psychologist's impression was definite that this child was aphasic. It was also suspected that hearing was impaired and this indeed was found to be the case. A year later a repeat WISC revealed a Verbal IQ of 72 and Performance IQ of 107. He had developed speech but it was still so poor it was very difficult to understand him.

At age 10 he became quite listless in school and seemed to be making involuntary jerking movements. A repeat EEG showed a shifting temporal focus of 6 Hz positive spiking. Diphenylhydantoin was prescribed and this had a dramatic effect of removing his listlessness and the jerking movements. His learning also increased in rate at this time. At age 13 a repeat WISC was almost identical to the previous one. About this time he was examined by several specialists in dyslexia all of whom agreed that he had a severe aphasia associated with some kind of brain damage. None of the usual medications, including d-amphetamine, methylphenidate, imipramine, acetazolamide, and methsuximide, had been effective with this child, and only when he began to have some kind of mild seizure was diphenylhydantoin effective. At this point it did make a major change in this boy's ability to function.

For several years he was in a learning disability class, but by junior high school he was able to go into a regular classroom, where he did quite well in the lowest track. At age 16 medication was discontinued with no ill effects.

8

Theoretical Considerations

Pathogenesis

Most of the patients were treated with either methylphenidate, d-amphetamine, desipramine, and imipramine; a few were treated with r-amphetamine, amitriptyline, nortriptyline, isocarboxazid. All of these drugs have one known biochemical action in common: they increase the pool of available norepinephrine in the brain (Hanson, 1967; Schildkraut et al., 1967). There are several mechanisms by which these drugs create this effect, which might partly account for the variability in effectiveness of each drug for MBD in different patients. Because improvement in behavior and concentration, when it occurs, takes place so quickly—often in half an hour—the mechanism of action must be directly biochemical, and this implies that the defect in MBD is biochemical. Since norepinephrine is a neurotransmitter, one can theorize that in MBD there are areas of defective impulse transmission from one neuron to another at synapses, resulting in faulty transmission or non-transmission of messages part of the time.

Since most of the brain is concerned with inhibitory messages, which are part of the negative feedback mechanisms of control systems, it is likely that if messages in general were lost in transmission, the major effect would be a disruption of negative feedback, leading to disrupted control systems. A great deal of what is clinically observable in MBD children is certainly subsumed in this category of disrupted control systems. For example, the "hyperkinetic" child is no more active on the playground than any other child, but when asked to sit still in church or school, the control of his musculature proves defective.*

Since anti-convulsants at times work as dramatically as the norepinephrine enhancers, some mechanism that responds equally quickly must be postulated. If one remembers that spikes and spike-waves are sudden electrical discharges from and in the brain, and that seizures result when the voltage of these discharges is sufficiently high to cross the insulation barrier and spread over large areas of the brain, then one can visualize electrical discharges not of sufficient voltage to cause seizures but, nevertheless, of sufficiently high voltage to disrupt messages being sent in the vicinity of these discharges. One can theorize, therefore, that eliminating or modulating the electrical discharges will improve the transmission of messages and hence improve the clinical picture. Whether the norepinephrine enhancers also have some effect via this mechanism is not known, but the high incidence of EEG abnormalities in MBD children suggests that this might be the case. There is also some evidence that anti-convulsants may enhance neurotransmission at synapses. This has definitely been

---

* Wender (1971) has made some interesting suppositions regarding the effect of medications via conditioning and reinforcement processes which depend on monoamines (dopamine, norepinephrine, serotonin). See also Randrup and Munkvad (1969), Scheckel et al. (1969), and Gazzaniga (1973). Coleman (1971) has found an increase of serotonin in blood platelets in hyperkinetic children, as compared to normal levels, and a decrease in serotonin as hyperactivity decreased. Corson et al. (1971) have reported the tranquilizing effect of d-amphetamine in hyperkinetic dogs.

demonstrated for diphenylhydantoin (Brumlik and Moretti, 1966).

In children with clinical evidence of brain damage (which frequently might be described more accurately as brain dysplasia) where there are anatomical as well as physiological defects, one would expect norepinephrine enhancers and anticonvulsants to be less effective and more reliance would have to be placed on the major tranquilizers. Indeed, the data demonstrate this (Table 27, p. 76). Also noteworthy is the fact that cases with "irritative phenomenon," such as spikes and spike-waves in the EEG, seem to show a much greater response to medication than cases with evidence of tissue damage (slow waves). Unfortunately, there are only five cases of the latter in our series.

How the physiologic disturbances improve with age and actually totally or partially heal by adolescence is not clear, but this improvement does follow the pattern of other brain disturbances, such as cerebral palsy, which gradually improve until a plateau is reached in adolescence.

Etiology

We have already demonstrated that it is common for more than one child in a family to have MBD, and we have shown that often there is a family history of a similar problem. When several members of a family are affected, they are usually affected to a different degree and in a somewhat different way. Yet, they are clearly distinguishable from the non-MBD children. For this reason, we conclude that for most MBD children, the etiology is a genetic disturbance. Other researchers have demonstrated genetic relationships in EEG abnormalities (Petersen and Akesson, 1968; Rodin, 1964) as well as suggestive genetic relationships between MBD and other psychiatric illness (Cantwell, 1972). It is difficult to explain the differences observed in our monozygotic twins. Most simply but least plausibly, they could be accounted for by environmental differences after conception. It is conceivable, but not possible to demonstrate at this stage of knowledge, that the differences are due to ambiguities in genetic coding, so that part of the time, by chance alone, coding is accurate, and part of the time inaccurate. Thus, when there is early splitting of the zygote into two fetuses, they may have somewhat different genetic material. Even when both twins had MBD, they were considerably different in their learning and behavior problems (Cases #442-443, p. 126 and #1011-1012, p. 115).

Other etiologies were undoubtedly present in our series, but were quantitatively of less importance. They include Thalidomide during pregnancy, rubella during pregnancy, prematurity, encephalitis, Klinefelter's syndrome, malnutrition, erythroblastosis fetalis, chorea, microcephaly, galactosemia, carbon monoxide poisoning, and difficult birth. These total less than 5% of our series.

Significance of the Electroencephalogram

Since the nature of the electrical output of the normal brain is largely a mystery, it should be no surprise that those changes in voltage and frequency we call abnormalities should also be shrouded in mystery. Over the years, purely empirically, certain abnormalities became associated with certain clinical features. Their relationships to epilepsy and to brain lesions have been carefully worked out, but correlations with psychiatric conditions have only recently been elucidated.

The most controversial dysrhythmia today is the 6 Hz or mixed 14 Hz and 6 Hz positive spike phenomenon discovered by Gibbs and Gibbs (1951). Lombroso et al. (1966) consider these spikes a normal feature of adolescence, and indeed, in most control series they are most common at puberty. But Gibbs and Gibbs (1963) consider them evidence of a thalamic epileptoid disorder. Indeed there is considerable evidence of neurovegetative disorders—but not the classical forms of epilepsy—associated with the 14/6 Hz phenomenon (Hughes, 1965; Hughes et al., 1965; Kellaway et al., 1959). Closely related to 14/6 Hz positive spike phenomenon are the 6 Hz positive spike-waves. The latter are usually found in the waking state, while the 14/6 Hz spikes are almost invariably found only in drowsiness and sleep. Why they are found so commonly in apparently normal children is the subject of much controversy, but we have demonstrated that the incidence in well-selected "normal" children is quite low.

Gianturco et al. (1972) described improvement in autonomic symptomatology with anticonvulsants, but not in psychiatric symptoms. Although Milstein and Small (1971) found only very subtle psychological correlates with 14/6 Hz spikes and 6 Hz positive spike-waves, Hughes et al. (1965) found more psychological disturbance with 6 Hz positive spike-waves than with other dysrhythmias. Both Hughes et al. (1961) and Gianturco et al. (1972) found combinations of behavioral and autonomic disturbances in their patients. A convincing report on the relevance of 14/6 Hz positive spiking to clinical phenomena was the case of Andy and Jurko (1972), a woman with intractable headache, irritable bowel, and emotional instability. An exploring electrode introduced in the anterior thalamic area revealed an active focus of 14 Hz positive spiking with propagation to the temporal and frontal cortex. An electrolytic lesion resulted in the complete alleviation of her complaints.

In our series, the most common EEG abnormality was the 6 or 14/6 Hz positive spike pattern. If to this is added the 6 Hz positive spike-wave pattern, half the total abnormalities found are accounted for. Since the improvement rate for treatment is the same for all the EEG abnormalities (except slow waves), it is inconceivable that these positive spike patterns have no clinical significance. Our control series and family studies do indeed indicate that infrequently these dysrhythmias are found in asymptomatic individuals, but the six-fold incidence in patients as compared to controls makes it prudent to accept these dysrhythmias as clinically significant if found in symptomatic individuals.

The other dysrhythmias have a more classical tradition in neurology, but in psychiatry there is still little acceptance of their significance, except in frank psychomotor seizures. Yet, the relationship of temporal lobe negative spikes to violence, to pathologic intoxication, and to other behavior disturbance has been amply demonstrated (Gross, 1971). Spike-wave and spike patterns may, without producing seizures, interfere with normal thought processes and with emotional control (Case #626, p. 132 is a good example). We believe dysrhythmias can best be thought of as signs of cerebral malfunctioning, the nature and degree being different for each case.

9

Conclusions

Our data lead us to the conclusion that MBD, loosely defined as it may be, represents a real entity with a specific treatment program. Major factors in distinguishing MBD from non-MBD children are those associated with (1) restlessness and (2) distractibility, although other defects in various control systems are often present. In MBD children, the EEG is abnormal more than half the time, as compared to a 5% incidence of abnormal EEG in controls. Psychological tests frequently but not variably demonstrate significant defects in perception. Examination in the usual office situation may reveal fidgetiness and a tendency to rush through tasks, but not always. Observation in a more stressful setting, such as the classroom, will be much more revealing; frequently the best history is obtained from the teacher.

We must also conclude that MBD is a very common disorder, possibly the most common psychiatric disorder of children. It is surely remarkable that three-quarters of over a thousand consecutive child patients were found to have this disorder. Certainly it is possible that the true prevalence of this disorder is less than these figures imply, and the large numbers of such patients referred to us involve some kind of artifact. One possibility is that a reputation for treating certain types of patients leads to an increase in referrals of just such a type of patient. However, if one can assume that there is a direct relation between an abnormal EEG and the incidence of MBD, we find that for the first two years of our project 54.1% of 122 patients had an abnormal EEG, while for the total population of 1056 over 9 years, the figure is 53.8%. This would tend to refute the explanation that we have seen more and more MBD children to the exclusion of non-MBD children over the years.

It is not unlikely, however, that the uniformity of our population base—almost entirely lower-middle and middle-middle class—has something to do with the kinds of problems most likely to lead to a referral to a mental health center. It is also true that, as mentioned earlier, the school referral system keeps many non-MBD patients for treatment by social workers and counselors within the school system, while MBD children are referred out as soon as MBD is suspected, since there is no medical diagnostic or treatment program within the school system.

Another factor may be the skill of teachers and counselors in spotting MBD, which may have developed almost immediately after our project was begun. Nevertheless, a comparison with another mental health center which also obtained routine EEG's for one year (see footnote, p. 39) reveals that they found an incidence of 42% with EEG abnormalities—a figure a fifth lower than ours, but still of the same order of magnitude. It is possible, therefore, that other practitioners who do not see such a high incidence of MBD in their child patients may be (1) serving a population base with quite different characteristics, (2) serving a school system which provides less counseling or therapy for its children, (3) missing the diagnosis of MBD in patients with less florid MBD symptoms.*

The EEG is useful in reinforcing one's clinical impression of MBD, but it is too crude a test in its present form to be relied on totally. Probably a therapeutic trial of medication is the most convincing approach to this disorder. Treatment with norepinephrine enhancers or anti-convulsants may produce dramatic improvement; significant improvement occurs in at least 80% of cases when various medications and dosage levels are pursued.

Counseling with parents and teachers is also of benefit since simply some knowledge of the nature of a patient's problem usually leads to greater efficacy of handling. Parents and teachers tend to blame themselves when things go wrong, and freedom from improperly placed guilt has immense therapeutic consequences all by itself.

MBD symptoms may be divided into two categories: behavior problems and learning problems. Most MBD children have some of each, but some may be found with predominantly one or the other. There is a natural tendency for these difficulties to improve with time, even without specific treatment. For milder cases, the outcome is very good with or without treatment. Treatment can improve the comfort of the child and those he is in contact with, and increase his learning. For cases of moderate severity, treatment can mean the difference between being a happy or a miserable person, having a happy or a miserable family, learning fairly well or losing interest in learning. For severe cases, treatment can mean the difference between normality and delinquency, com-

---

* In training psychiatric residents, we found that they were skeptical of the diagnosis of MBD unless the patient was severely hyperactive—that is, fidgety and restless during the examination. Many residents were quite resistive to prescribing a trial of medication for patients who, to us, were classically MBD, and they were frequently astounded at favorable responses and gratitude from the family. This resistance was just as noticeable in residents who chose our facility for training because they wanted experience in the diagnosis and treatment of MBD.

pleting school and dropping out, being a respectable member of society and being a criminal.

The medications used most commonly, methylphenidate, d-amphetamine, desipramine, and imipramine, are quite safe to use. Mild side effects occur in about one in eight or nine patients, but these do not warrant discontinuing the medication. Moderate and severe side effects occur in one of sixteen patients, but these effects quickly subside in a day or two and another medication can be tried. No long-term side effects were observable other than anorexia, weight loss, and occasional slowing of growth in height.

Although some patients improved on several different medications, most did better on one than on the others. Which one turned out to work best seemed totally unpredictable. If one had to choose an order in which they should be tried, it would be more or less as follows: methylphenidate, desipramine or imipramine, d-amphetamine, diphenylhydantoin, thioridazine, haloperidol. When tics are present, they are frequently made worse by the stimulants, but haloperidol will help control them. When subtle seizures are present, a variety of anticonvulsants should be tried.

The earlier the syndrome is detected and treated, the better the results, and the simpler the treatment. For younger children, psychotherapy is neither necessary nor helpful. For older children, and especially early adolescents, when habit patterns have already been well established, some dyadic or group therapy may be indicated. Usually, however, working with parents, individually or in groups, is far more effective than psychotherapy directly with the child.

MBD is found at all ages in childhood, and at all IQ levels. Some children with frank brain damage, with or without mental retardation, also benefit from pharmacotherapy.

10

Current Concepts of Diagnosis and Therapy

Inasmuch as MBD is such a common disorder, it should be suspected in every child who has a behavior or learning problem, no matter how mild or severe. The history, as with most medical problems, is crucial. A questionnaire can be useful in eliciting symptoms very quickly, and we have included the one we currently use in Appendix F.* The history will almost always include distractibility and short attention span, especially in school, as well as restlessness, a tendency to be "on the go" all the time, impulsiveness, explosiveness. The problems may be behavioral or learning or both. The complaints may center mostly around the home or mostly around the school, or may be present in both. Often complaints involve only situations in which the child is stimulated. Occasionally, complaints are limited to "overreactions" to stress.

The interview with the parents is also revealing. The parents often seem much better integrated than parents of non-

---

* This questionnaire may be reproduced if desired for one's clinical use.

MBD children, although of course an MBD child may be found in a disturbed home too. Often one is impressed that other children in the family do very well; in fact, this can commonly be seen in the waiting room as one observes how the patient and siblings who happen to be brought along behave there. One looks also for a family history of the same problem or similar ones. Often it is found that a child has the same problem getting along with mother, father, teacher, baby sitter or grandmother indiscriminately, while with non-MBD children, it is more common to find more severe disturbances relating to one person than to another. One obtains the history of how both parents were raised, looking for similarities in the way they were brought up and the way they treat their children: frequently one finds a discrepancy between the way the parents handle the children and the way the children react, that is, the children frequently appear to overreact.

Young children may be observed in a playroom or given toys to play with in the office to determine how they relate to the toys as well as to the examiner. Asking the children to draw with crayons is frequently fruitful, for most children like to draw and one can chat with them more comfortably while they draw, for they do not feel so much "on the spot." The way they go about their drawings, their attention span, use or lack of color, the care or hastiness with which they approach the task, and the content of what they draw are all revealing. They can also be asked to draw a standard drawing such as the Draw-A-Person or House-Tree-Person or Draw-Your-Family-Doing-Something test. These can be saved and compared with other drawings done at a subsequent time.

Older children often enjoy drawing too, or at least can be persuaded to make a drawing. They may prefer doing something rather than just sitting and talking. They may have no insight into their behavior, assuming only that they are picked on for no good reason. How much a child reveals verbally depends, of course, on the child and on the skill of the examiner; naturally, with children we depend a great deal on nonverbal communication.

It should be emphasized that in the playroom or office MBD children may be quiet and calm and display none of the behavior complained about. However, a certain hypomanic quality is frequently present—the child relates "too easily." Fantasies tend to be grandiose, such as wishing for "all the money in the world."

A full neurological examination should be done with emphasis on large and small muscle coordination, gait, muscle tone and spasticity. Watching a child go up and down stairs can be very revealing.

Psychological tests are essential for children with learning problems, and may be helpful for children with behavior problems. While there is no agreement among psychologists on exactly what tests are useful for diagnosing learning problems, one should certainly not give much credence to group testing and insist on individual testing. The Bender-Gestalt and the Wechsler Intelligence Scale for Children or Wechsler Pre-Primer Scale of Intelligence for very young children should be considered a minimum, for many other IQ tests rely heavily on verbal skills and may miss the problem of the child with poor verbal and good non-verbal skills or vice versa. The psychologist provides an independent measure of the child's restlessness and distractibility and his approach to tasks, as well as data on skills and handicaps as revealed by the various sub-tests. But it must be remembered that the usual psychological signs of "organicity" will not be present in MBD.

An EEG is of some use as a guide to therapy. Negative spikes and spike-waves lead one to consider anti-convulsants, whereas positive spikes and spike-waves lead one to consider the stimulants first. Slow waves should make one cautious about any help at all from pharmacotherapy and may steer one ultimately to the phenothiazines or butyrophenones. It must be remembered that a sleep record is essential and that a normal EEG does not prove that there are no abnormalities in the brain. If the clinical and EEG data point to MBD, a trial of medication is certainly indicated. If one is skeptical, a placebo given for a week or two followed by active medication will give more conclusive results, although it must be realized that the optimum medication and optimum dosage cannot be determined in advance and some trial and error must be involved.

The parents are told that it is likely or possible that the child suffers from a brain dysfunction (not "damage" which is a much more frightening term, unless damage actually exists) which he will probably outgrow sometime in adolescence, but which, in the meantime, puts him under a handicap. We emphasize the most important consequence is damage to a child's self-image; by doing poorly in school, by being scolded all the time, or by whatever this particular child does which leads to a poor self-concept, he grows to dislike himself. We emphasize that many things can be learned later in life or not learned at all without creating misery. But a poor self-image has lifelong consequences which can never be really erased.

The dysfunction can be likened to immaturity in some part of the brain or deficiency of some chemical necessary in brain functioning, or, to more sophisticated parents, to a defect in neurotransmission which results in problems in learning and in control systems. A useful analogy is a car with defective brakes. At 10 miles per hour, the defect is not important, but at 60 miles per hour it indeed becomes important. Thus, a child not under stress can behave quite normally, but under stress may show dyscontrol and maladaptive behavior. Typical stresses are teasing, angry feelings, presence of several other children, loud noises, wild games, absence of or distance from controlling adults, new situations, difficult tasks, fatigue, confusion, attempting to do too many things at once. Counter measures are structure, quiet, closeness of controlling adult, firmness, stopping out-of-control behavior when it starts and not after it has reached the exploding point, limiting the number of children present, easing gradually into new situations, keeping the number of tasks to a quantity he can handle at one time, keeping the difficulty of tasks to a level he can reasonably master.

Parents are told that medication often helps, sometimes dramatically, and that the risks from medication are slight, and the risk of addiction is zero, while the benefits can be very great. Unless one uses placebo first, methylphenidate is probably the first drug which should be tried unless enuresis or encopresis is present or unless the child is post-pubertal, when desipramine or imipramine is more likely to be helpful. If medication is not helpful but creates no ill effects, the dosage should be increased until it is clear that no benefits can ensue, at which time another drug should be tried. After methylphenidate and des/imipramine have been tried, the amphetamines, diphenylhydantoin, thioridazine, or haloperidol should be tried. Sometimes a combination works best, for example, methylphenidate and thioridazine. The guide to drug dosage outlined on page 21 can be used.

Methylphenidate is usually sufficient given in the morning and after lunch, but when symptoms recur in the evening, an after-school dose, usually smaller than the morning dose, is indicated. Sometimes this dose does not last until bedtime, and an after-supper dose should be given. Occasionally, a dose before bedtime is necessary to enable a child to settle down properly for sleep, but this is not common. Not uncommonly, the morning dose necessary to enable a child to get through the entire morning efficiently is so large that when the child first gets to school he feels strange or lethargic. In such a case, it is best to give a smaller morning dose and to have someone at school administer a mid-morning dose. Sometimes, for similar reasons, a mid-afternoon dose is necessary. Occasionally a child is so difficult in the morning hours, before the morning dose has had time to take effect, that it has been found desirable to awake him about an hour before his usual waking time, have him take the medication and return to sleep. Then when he awakes the methylphenidate is already at work.

D-amphetamine never requires such frequent dosage. Tablets are usually administered in the morning and at lunch, occasionally with a third dose later in the day. The time-disintegration capsules usually suffice with one dose each morning.

Des/imipramine can usually be given in one dose at bedtime, but sometimes it can be observed to be losing its effect in the afternoon or evening, in which case twice-a-day dosage will improve the results. This also applies to thioridazine. Diphenylhydantoin and haloperidol require two to four doses daily.

When after a time symptoms recur, the first thought should be of increasing the dosage. Some children use the same dose until it is discontinued in adolescence, others require increases two or three times a year.

Phenobarbital is absolutely contraindicated; it almost always makes MBD symptoms worse. Patients receiving phenobarbital can be materially helped simply by discontinuing this medication. The situation is more complicated when epilepsy requires the use of phenobarbital, or of mephobarbital (Mebaral) or primidone (Mysoline), both of which are metabolized to phenobarbital in the body. Sometimes these medications can be gradually replaced by non-barbiturates, without jeopardizing control of seizures. This measure often reduces MBD symptoms.

Parents should be asked to make careful observations, and teachers should also be asked to contribute their observations when the problems involve the school. Calls to or conferences with the teacher, psychologist, or school counselor are often helpful. A good relationship with the school is well worth cultivating. If medication works well, parents should be advised that an increase in dosage will be necessary from time to time, and if some of the original symptoms recur, all that may be needed is a larger dose. Children may not need to be seen often, as little as once in six months, if all appears to be going well.

Generally it is advisable to maintain the use of medication on weekends and holidays, even though the main problem is in school. One reason is that children learn when they are out of school as well as in, and this should not be hampered in any way; another is that medication maintains some effect for several days, and if stopped on weekends, there will be a lower level on Mondays. Occasionally a child will do well on medication but some anorexia persists, leading to inadequate caloric intake. Such a child can be helped by a high protein diet using skim milk powder to make double-strength skim milk, which is usually quite acceptable to a child, even if he is not too hungry, and encouraging a bedtime snack. Medication can be skipped on weekends and holidays, since in this case the nutrition becomes an important factor. Cyproheptadine (Periactin), one tablet taken three times daily, will also often help the appetite. It is advisable to plot a growth curve for children taking stimulants, to be sure that height and weight are progressing within acceptable limits.

Besides being given the medication, parents should be advised that the child lacks inner controls and that external controls are necessary to replace defective inner controls—to a much greater extent than with the normal child. Greater supervision and greater ingenuity in preventing foreseeable difficulties should be emphasized. For example, if in the car the patient is constantly stirring up trouble with siblings in the back seat, he should be made to sit in the front seat next to his parents. MBD children usually require more structure than others, have difficulty with new situations and prefer a regimen. They feel and behave best when they know someone firm is in charge.

When a child is well into adolescence, it should be anticipated that medication at some point will no longer be required. Usually from time to time every patient will forget his medication; failure of anyone to notice any difference is a clue that medication may no longer be needed. However, more than one day is needed to really evaluate this, and medication should be discontinued for a month, at which time a report is obtained from home and school. If no difference is noted, than it can be discontinued for another month or two and if again no difference is noted and grades in school are maintained, then it can be discontinued permanently. At times, the patient on stimulants, as mentioned before, will "outgrow" the drug but will still be restless and distractible, and such a patient will often do well on des/imipramine.

With adolescent children, there is a danger that they may attempt to distribute stimulants to friends at school if they have free access to them. For this age group, parents would do well to maintain some supervision and control, especially if amphetamines are used. In older children, if des/imipramine works as well as amphetamines, the former may be preferred since it has no marketability for illicit use.

Formal psychotherapy appears totally useless for younger children. If they are impulsive, they will continue to act first and think later. Working with parents and teachers is infinitely more effective. For older children, about 12 years and up, some direct psychotherapy or group therapy may be beneficial, when other modalities have failed or have been of less than optimal benefit. For the adolescent, the situation may demand some individual attention to the child. Although for our series we were unable to provide psychotherapy for adolescents, there were a number of cases in which we would have liked to have had psychotherapy, especially group therapy, at our disposal. The adolescent may already be beyond the state where he can be benefited adequately by working with parents and teachers and relying on pharmacotherapy. Even so, we have found that many of our patients, even older ones, have had psychotherapy or counseling by others to no avail, only to respond remarkably to pharmacotherapy. So for the great bulk of MBD patients, formal psychotherapy is definitely not indicated.

Glossary

Albuminuria: Albumin in the urine, usually indicative of kidney disease.

Alpha waves or alpha rhythm: One of the fundamental waves of the electroencephalogram. It ranges in frequency from 8 to 13 cycles per second in adults, somewhat slower in children, is associated maximally with the occipital (back) regions of the brain; it is reduced in activity by physiological stimuli, particularly vision (opening the eyes). (See illustration in Appendix G.)

Aminoaciduria: A rare condition in which amino acids appear in the urine, reflecting a metabolic abnormality.

Anorexia: Loss of appetite.

Anticonvulsants: Medications used to control convulsive seizures or epilepsy; they may also help in non-convulsive conditions.

Anti-Parkinson drug: A medication used to neutralize the tendency of certain tranquilizers to produce symptoms similar to those found in Parkinson's disease.

Aphasia: A disorder of the brain in which the centers for language are affected. Aphasia can occur in someone of normal intelligence, yet he will have more or less difficulty in the use of language in any of its forms: speaking, writing, or the appreciation of the written or spoken word.

Apraxia: A disorder of voluntary movement, consisting in a defect in capacity to execute purposeful movements, notwithstanding the preservation of muscular power, sensibility, and coordination in general.

Asymptomatic: Having no symptoms.

Autism, autistic: A mental condition or symptom in which a person is absorbed in himself to an extent that his thoughts and ideas become private and bizarre and not understandable to others.

Autonomic: Pertaining to that part of the nervous system governing automatic functions which go on without conscious control, such as digestion.

Bender-Gestalt test: A test for visual-motor skills, involving the copying of standardized series of designs.

Bifrontal: Referring to both sides of the front of the head or brain.

Bitemporal: Referring to both sides of the region of the temples of the head or brain.

Breech delivery: The birth of a baby feet or buttocks first instead of the usual head first.

Catecholamines: Natural substances produced in the body which perform a variety of functions. In the brain they appear essential for normal brain functioning. Two commonly studied catecholamines are norepinephrine and serotonin.

Chi square (χ^2)*:* A statistical computation used in determining "statistical significance" (see "p").

Chorea: A disease related to rheumatic fever; the brain is affected, and this produces twisting, jerking movements, which subside after a time.

Colic: In infants, a severe indigestion resulting in crying and screaming. It usually subsides by 6 months of age.

Commissure: A structure containing nerve fibres connecting the right and left cerebral hemispheres.

Control: In statistical and research parlance, a "normal" group used to compare with groups being studied for some disease or problem.

Correlation coefficient ("r"): A statistical measure of the relationship between two variables. A high value of "r" indicates that the two variables are closely related.

Cortical: Referring to the cerebral cortex, or outer part of the main portion of the brain. Highest mental functioning takes place in the cortex.

Cybernetics: The study of automatic control systems in the brain, using mechanical analogies such as computers.

Delirious: Referring to an alteration in consciousness in which the patient is disoriented, incoherent, and mentally clouded.

Diastolic pressure: Blood pressure during maximal relaxation of the heart.

Diphasic spike: A pattern on the electroencephalogram in which there is a sudden burst of electricity first in a negative direction and then in a positive direction (see illustration in Appendix G).

Double-blind: A pattern for a research study to test the effectiveness of a medication. The patient is given either an active medication or an identical looking sugar pill, coded so that neither the patient nor the doctor know which is which. Thus pre-judgment or suggestion cannot enter into the evaluation. Only the head of the research project has the key to the code, and he does not break the code until the data are complete. If the active medication helps a certain percentage of the patients, but the inert "medicine" helps just about the same percentage, it is likely that the effect of both is only by the power of suggestion. On the other hand, if the active medication is clearly superior to the inert "medicine," this superiority can be considered real and valid.

Dyadic: Referring to a one-to-one relationship.

Dyslexia: Severe difficulty learning to read in a person of otherwise normal ability.

Dysplasia: Abnormal tissue development.

Dysrhythmia: An abnormal rhythm or wave formation in the electroencephalogram.

Dystonia: A condition in which there are involuntary twisting movements of muscles. It is an occasional side effect of certain tranquilizers, as well as a symptom of Parkinson's disease.

Electroencephalogram (EEG): A recording of the electrical output of the brain, usually the outer surface of the brain. Ten or more disc-shaped electrodes are attached to various parts of the scalp by means of a paste, and the electrodes are connected to a high-fidelity amplifier, which in turn drives a series of pens on a strip of paper. To be complete, an electrocephalogram should be recorded while the patient is both awake and sleep.

Electrolytic: The destruction of small areas of tissue by an electric current.

Encephalitis: Inflammation of the brain; "brain fever."

Encopresis: Involuntary passage of feces.

Enuresis: Involuntary passage of urine, usually while asleep.

Epilepsy: A condition in which there are periodic attacks of unconsciousness or alterations in consciousness. The attacks may be extremely brief (a second) or prolonged (several minutes). Sometimes there are convulsions—violent involuntary muscular contractions—sometimes not. There are dozens of kinds of epilepsy, all with different symptoms.

Erythroblastosis fetalis: "Rh disease," in which the child's red blood cells are destroyed during pregnancy, leaving him severely jaundiced at birth, with possible brain damage.

Estrangement: The sensation of not feeling "like oneself," a strange feeling of having suddenly become different and distant.

Fast waves: On the electroencephalogram, waves of 14 to 25 cycles per second. When these waves are of very high amplitude, they are abnormal. Fast waves are also called Beta waves (see illustration in Appendix G).

Febrile seizures: A fairly common condition in infants and very young children, in which very high fevers induce convulsions.

Frontal: Referring to the front of the head or brain.

Formication: The delusional feeling that insects are crawling over one or just under the skin.

Fourteen-and-six Hz positive spikes: A pattern on the electroencephalogram, usually observed in drowsiness and sleep, in which there are sudden bursts of positive electricity giving the appearance of a "spike," arising at a mixed frequency of 14 per second and 6 per second. These patterns are thought to arise from deep structures within the brain (see illustration in Appendix G).

Galactosemia: The presence of an abnormal sugar in the bloodstream, due to an inborn defect. Ordinarily a child born with this disease becomes mentally retarded, but with special diets this can be avoided.

Genetic: Traits transmitted from parents to offspring by genetic units called genes. There are two genes for every trait, one coming from each parent. Often if one gene is defective, the other (normal) gene takes over, and no abnormal trait is seen. But if both genes have some defect, an abnormal trait will be seen.

Grand mal: Refers to (1) a severe convulsion in which consciousness is lost and there is a violent contraction of all the body muscles; (2) repeated spike activity in the electroencephalogram, often *but not always* associated with grand mal convulsions.

Hemisphere: One or the other side of the cerebrum, or main part of the brain.

Hertz (Hz): A term meaning cycles per second.

Hyperkinesis, hyperkinetic: Excessive activity; hyperactivity.

Hypertension: High blood pressure.

Hyperventilation: During the recording of the electroencephalogram, the patient is asked to breathe deeply for about 3 minutes. This produces subtle changes in the blood, which in turn brings out certain abnormalities which might not otherwise appear.

Insomnia: Difficulty falling asleep and/or staying asleep.

Klinefelter's syndrome: A disease affecting males only, in which masculine traits are poorly developed. It is due to an extra X-chromosome.

Larval grand mal discharges: On the electroencephalogram, very short bursts of spike discharges suggestive of grand mal tendency.

Lesion: A more or less circumscribed abnormal condition of a tissue.

MAO inhibitors: Medications which inhibit an enzyme called "monoamine oxidase." This enzyme destroys catecholamines. Therefore, any medication which inhibits this enzyme will slow down the destruction of catecholamines, and thus increase their availability in the brain.

Maple syrup urine disease: A rare disease in which there is an inborn error of metabolism. The urine has a maple syrup odor.

Microcephaly: A head smaller than normal, usually associated with an abnormally small brain.

Minimal brain dysfunction (MBD): A condition of children in which there is some evidence of some malfunctioning of the brain, but not enough malfunctioning to produce clearcut evidence such as might be seen in children with gross brain damage, as with cerebral palsy.

Mode, modal: In statistics, that value of a variable corresponding to the greatest frequency of that variable in the entire distribution. It differs from "average" in that the latter is unduly influenced by extreme values, whereas the mode refers to a central clustering of values, unaffected by extremes.

Monozygotic: Arising from one egg; applied to twins. The same as "identical" twins.

Negative: Used in two ways: (1) meaning normal, or no abnormalties found; (2) meaning negative electricity, as opposed to positive.

Negative spikes: A pattern on the electroencephalogram in which there is a sudden burst of negative electricity, appearing like a spike. This pattern is thought to arise from the surface parts of the brain (see illustration in Appendix G).

Negative spike-waves: A pattern on the electroencephalogram in which there is a sudden burst of negative electricity, appearing like a "spike" on the record, followed by a slow wave (see illustration in Appendix G).

Neurologic signs: Changes in sensation, muscular strength, muscular coordination, and reflexes, indicating some gross malfunction of the brain and/or the rest of the nervous system. Also called "hard" neurologic signs, to distinguish from "soft" signs, which are more equivocal.

Neurophysiology: The science of the function of the nervous system.

Neurosis: A mental or emotional disorder in which there is no recognized structural defect in the brain and no loss of contact with reality. Anxiety states, phobias, and some depressions are typical neuroses.

Neurotransmission: The process whereby a signal or message in one nerve is passed on to another nerve.

Neurotransmitter: A substance, believed to be norepinephrine, which allows messages or signals to be transmitted from one nerve to another in the brain.

Neurovegetative: Pertaining to the autonomic nervous system, which governs automatic functions which go on without conscious control, such as breathing, digestion, perspiration.

Night terrors: A condition observed in young children fairly frequently. They suddenly scream during the night as though paralyzed with fear, and need several minutes of comforting to "come to" and relax. Night terrors are not the same as nightmares.

Norepinephrine: One of the catecholamines in the brain, believed to be responsible for the transmission of messages from one nerve to another.

Notched waves: A pattern on the electroencephalogram in which a slow wave (usually 6 Hz) has a depression or notch in it (see illustration in Appendix G).

Occipital: Refers to the back of the head or brain.

Organicity: The presence of organic brain disease, as opposed to "emotional problems."

Orthostatic hypotension: Excessively low blood pressure noted immediately upon standing up from a lying or sitting position, leading to faintness for a few seconds or minutes, or to actual fainting.

"p": This refers to "probability" in statistics. If p is less than ($<$) 0.05, it means that there is less than 5 chances in 100 that

the results obtained could have come from random variation alone. (If one flipped a coin 10 times and it came out heads 7 times, one could not conclude that something was wrong with the coin. This result could arise from chance alone even if the coin were perfectly balanced. If p were calculated it would be very much greater than 0.05.) If p is less than 0.05, scientists give good credence to the validity of the results, which are said to be "statistically significant." If p is less than 0.01, excellent credence is given. If p is greater than 0.05, the results might still be valid, but there is a suspicion that the results *could* have come out that way because of chance variation (as with the coin).

Parietal: Referring to the side of the head or brain.

Pathologic intoxication: The production of severe behavior abnormalities by only small amounts of alcohol—amounts far smaller than would be required to produce drunkenness.

Perception: The mental process by which data from the sense organs are recognized as something meaningful.

Perceptual defect: A defect in the ability of the brain to process sensory data into something meaningful. If there is an auditory perceptual defect, it is presumed that the ears function adequately, but the brain has difficulty in processing what the ears hear into something meaningful.

Perseveration: Not perseverance, which is a useful trait, but the aimless, compulsive repetition of some activity long after its usefulness is gone.

Petit mal: A variety of seizure in which consciousness is lost for only very brief periods, resulting in staring and losing track of what one has been doing or saying, but not falling or convulsing.

Pharmacotherapy: Treatment with medicines.

Placebo: A "dummy" pill or capsule made of an inert material, usually milk sugar, but fashioned to look like an active medication.

Platelets: A component of the blood necessary for clotting.

Projective tests: Psychological tests in which vague and unstructured test material is presented to the patient, who then "projects" into the test material his own fantasies, worries, or problems. Used for personality assessment.

Psychogenic: Caused by psychological or emotional problems.

Psychomotor seizures: Seizures in which consciousness is altered but not lost, the patient often acting in a peculiar way, with no memory later of what happened.

Psychosis: A mental disorder in which there is a significant loss of contact with reality.

Retardation, mental retardation: A condition in which intelligence is impared to such a degree that a child cannot be expected to function in a regular classroom. Retardation can vary from very mild to very severe. The milder forms permit a child to be educated to some degree (educable mentally handicapped); he can learn to read, write, count, work at simple tasks, and generally function in society without supervision when he grows up. Moderate retardation (trainable mentally handicapped) does not permit true education, but a child can be trained to take care of his personal needs, such as dressing himself. When he grows up he will need some sort of supervision. Severe retardation is not compatible with any social functioning.

Rubella: German measles. If a mother contracts rubella during the first part of pregnancy, the likelihood of serious abnormalities in the child is substantial.

Seizure: This term is used in two ways: (1) it describes attacks of unconsciousness, with or without convulsions; or alterations of consciousness, or peculiar sensations or peculiar behavior which come in periodic spells; (2) it describes patterns on the electroencephalogram often, *but not necessarily,* associated with the attacks listed under (1).

Serotonin: One of the catecholamines in the brain and other parts of the body.

Sharp waves: On the electroencephalogram, abnormal waves which are almost shaped like spikes but are somewhat rounded.

Sibling: A brother or sister.

Single-blind: A research study to test the effectiveness of medication. The patient can be given either active medication or an inert "medicine." If, with many trials, the active medicine is clearly superior to the inert "medicine," this superiority can be considered real and valid, since the patient does not know whether the medication he received was active or inactive, or even that any inactive material was used; thus the role of suggestion is eliminated. However, since the doctor or other evaluator knows which is which, he might be prejudiced in his evaluation. A "double-blind" program, where neither patent nor evaluator knows which medicine is active or inactive, is therefore more elegant than a single-blind study.

Six Hz positive spikes: A pattern on the electroencephalogram, usually observed in drowsiness and sleep, in which there are sudden bursts of positive electricity giving the appearance of a "spike," arising at a frequency of six per second. This pattern is thought to arise from deep structures within the brain (see illustration in Appendix G).

Six Hz positive spike-waves: An electroencephalographic pattern, usually found in the waking state, in which there are sudden bursts of positive electricity (spike) followed by a wave at a rhythm of six per second. This pattern is thought to arise from deep structures within the brain (see illustration in Appendix G).

Sleep record: A recording of the electroencephalogram during sleep. Sleep brings out many abnormalities which do not appear in the waking state. Often sleep is induced by a small quantity of a sleeping medicine of a kind known not to effect the electroencephalogram.

Slow waves: On the electroencephalogram, waves 7 per second or slower. Some slow waves are normal during sleep, but definitely abnormal in a wake record, usually indicating depressed tissue function or damage (see illustration in Appendix G). Waves 4 to 7 per second are called Theta waves, and waves slower than 4 per second are called Delta waves.

Spasticity: A stiffness of muscles due to brain damage.

Synapse: A very small space between the end of one nerve fibre and the receiving part of another nerve: the space across which neurotransmission must take place for signals or messages to get through.

Systolic pressure: Blood pressure during maximal contraction of the heart.

Tachyphylaxis: Rapid production of immunity to a medicine.

Temporal: Refers to the area of the head or brain around the temples.

Thalamic: Pertaining to the thalamus, a part of the brain representing a very important coordination center.

Thalidomide: A sedative used in Europe for a time before it was discovered that its use in pregnant women resulted in severe birth defects.

Tic: A brief but repeated involuntary muscular twitch.

Tricyclic amines: A group of medicines which are believed to increase, in the brain, the available pool of catecholamines.

Visual-motor skills: The *mental* ability involved in coordinating what the eye sees with what the hand does.

Wechsler Intelligence Scale for Children (WISC): A psychological test consisting of several subtests, about half of them involving tests using verbal or language functions, the rest testing functions which do not depend on words or language (like assembling parts to make a whole). The former is averaged to a "Verbal IQ," the latter to a "Performance IQ," and the entire test is averaged to a "Full Scale IQ." The test is given individually, not in groups, so that the tester, who should be a qualified psychologist, can determine not only the actual scores, but the way the child goes about the testing, and what kinds of difficulties he encounters. Thus the test is more than a set of numbers, but a much more comprehensive assessment of a child's abilities.

Zygote: The fertilized egg.

Appendix A

Symptomatology—Identification of The Child

In a search for symptoms attributed to children with minimal brain dysfunctioning, over 100 recent publications were reviewed.

Many different terms were used to describe the same symptom, e.g., excessive motor activity for age might be referred to as any one of the following: hyperactivity, hyperkinesis, organic driveness, restlessness, motor obsessiveness, fidgetiness, motor disinhibition, or nervousness.

A large number of terms were too broad for other than limited value, e.g., "poor academic achievement"; others were more specific, e.g., "reading ability two grade levels below grade placement." A few are mentioned one time only, e.g., "inclined to have fainting spells." Others are too general (or judgmental) to classify, e.g., "often good looking." Opposite characteristics are common: "physically immature for age"—

Excerpted from Clements, S. D.: *Minimal Brain Dysfunction in Children. Terminology and Identification.* Phase One of a Three-Phase Project. U.S. Department of Health, Education, and Welfare, NINDB Monograph No. 3, 1966.

"physically advanced for age;" "fearless"—"phobic;" "outgoing"—"shy;" "hyperactive"—"hypoactive."

These examples represent some of the difficulties encountered in developing a scheme for classification of the symptoms, and indicate the variety of syndromes contained within the primary diagnosis of minimal brain dysfunctioning. The following represents an attempt to classify some of the descriptive elements culled from the literature.

PRELIMINARY CATEGORIES OF SIGNS AND SYMPTOMS

A. *Test Performance Indicators*

1. Spotty or patchy intellectual deficits. Achievement low in some areas; high in others.
2. Below mental age level on drawing tests (man, house, etc.).
3. Geometric figure drawings poor for age and measured intelligence.
4. Poor performance on block design and marble board tests.
5. Poor showing on group tests (intelligence and achievement) and daily classroom examinations which require reading.
6. Characteristic subtest patterns on the Wechsler Intelligence Scale for Children, including "scatter" within both Verbal and Performance Scales; high Verbal—low Performance; low Verbal—high Performance.

B. *Impairments of Perception and Concept-formation*

1. Impaired discrimination of size.
2. Impaired discrimination of right-left and up-down.
3. Impaired tactile discriminations.
4. Poor spatial orientation.
5. Impaired orientation in time.
6. Distorted concept of body image.
7. Impaired judgment of distance.
8. Impaired discrimination of figure-ground.
9. Impaired discrimination of part-whole.

10. Frequent perceptual reversals in reading and in writing letters and numbers.
11. Poor perceptual integration. Child cannot fuse sensory impressions into meaningful entities.

C. *Specific Neurologic Indicators*

1. Few, if any, apparent gross abnormalities.
2. Many "soft," equivocal, or borderline findings.
4. Frequency of mild visual or hearing impairments.
5. Strabismus.
6. Nystagmus.
7. High incidence of left, and mixed laterality and confused perception of laterality.
8. Hyperkinesis.
9. Hypokinesis.
10. General awkwardness.
11. Poor fine visual-motor coordination.

D. *Disorders of Speech and Communication*

1. Impaired discrimination of auditory stimuli.
2. Various categories of aphasia.
3. Slow language development.
4. Frequent mild hearing loss.
5. Frequent mild speech irregularities.

E. *Disorders of Motor Function*

1. Frequent athetoid, choreiform, tremulous, or rigid movements of hands.
2. Frequent delayed motor milestones.
3. General clumsiness or awkwardness.
4. Frequent tics and grimaces.
5. Poor fine or gross visual-motor coordination.
6. Hyperactivity.
7. Hypoactivity.

F. *Academic Achievement and Adjustment* (Chief complaints about the child by his parents and teachers)

1. Reading disabilities.
2. Arithmetic disabilities.
3. Spelling disabilities.
4. Poor printing, writing, or drawing ability.

    5. Variability in performance from day to day or even hour to hour.

    6. Poor ability to organize work.

    7. Slowness in finishing work.

    8. Frequent confusion about instructions, yet success with verbal tasks.

G. *Disorders of Thinking Processes*

    1. Poor ability for abstract reasoning.

    2. Thinking generally concrete.

    3. Difficulties in concept-formation.

    4. Thinking frequently disorganized.

    5. Poor short-term and long-term memory.

    6. Thinking sometimes autistic.

    7. Frequent thought perseveration.

H. *Physical Characteristics*

    1. Excessive drooling in the young child.

    2. Thumb-sucking, nail-biting, head-banging, and teeth-grinding in the young child.

    3. Food habits often peculiar.

    4. Slow to toilet train.

    5. Easy fatigability.

    6. High frequency of enuresis.

    7. Encopresis.

I. *Emotional Characteristics*

    1. Impulsive.

    2. Explosive.

    3. Poor emotional and impulse control.

    4. Low tolerance for frustration.

    5. Reckless and uninhibited; impulsive then remorseful.

J. *Sleep Characteristics*

    1. Body or head rocking before falling into sleep.

    2. Irregular sleep patterns in the young child.

    3. Excessive movement during sleep.

    4. Sleep abnormally light or deep.

    5. Resistance to naps and early bedtime, e.g., seems to require less sleep than average child.

K. *Relationship Capacities*

1. Peer group relationships generally poor.
2. Overexcitable in normal play with other children.
3. Better adjustment when playmates are limited to one or two.
4. Frequently poor judgment in social and interpersonal situations.
5. Socially bold and aggressive.
6. Inappropriate, unselective, and often excessive displays of affection.
7. Easy acceptance of others alternating with withdrawal and shyness.
8. Excessive need to touch, cling, and hold on to others.

L. *Variations of Physical Development*

1. Frequent lags in developmental milestones, e.g., motor, language, etc.
2. Generalized maturational lag during early school years.
3. Physically immature; or
4. Physical development normal or advanced for age.

M. *Characteristics of Social Behavior*

1. Social competence frequently below average for age and measured intelligence.
2. Behavior often inappropriate for situation, and consequences apparently not foreseen.
3. Possibly negative and aggressive to authority.
4. Possibly antisocial behavior.

N. *Variations of Personality*

1. Overly gullible and easily led by peers and older youngsters.
2. Frequent rage reactions and tantrums when crossed.
3. Very sensitive to others.
4. Excessive variation in mood and responsiveness from day to day and even hour to hour.
5. Poor adjustment to environmental changes.
6. Sweet and even tempered, cooperative and friendly (most commonly the so-called hypokinetic child).

O. *Disorders of Attention and Concentration*

   1. Short attention span for age.
   2. Overly distractible for age.
   3. Impaired concentration ability.
   4. Motor or verbal perseveration.
   5. Impaired ability to make decisions, particularly from
       many choices.

Several authors note that many of the characteristics tend
to improve with the normal maturation of the central nervous
system. As the child matures, various complex motor acts and
differentiations appear or are more easily acquired.

Variability beyond that expected for age and measured intelligence appears throughout most of the signs and symptoms.
This, of course, limits predictability and expands misunderstanding of the child by his parents, peers, teachers, and often
the clinicians who work with him.

Ten characteristics most often cited by the various authors,
in order of frequency:

   1. Hyperactivity.
   2. Perceptual-motor impairments.
   3. Emotional lability.
   4. General coordination deficits.
   5. Disorders of attention (short attention span, distrac-
       tibility, perseveration).
   6. Impulsivity.
   7. Disorders of memory and thinking.
   8. Specific learning disabilities:

       a. Reading.
       b. Arithmetic.
       c. Writing.
       d. Spelling.

   9. Disorders of speech and hearing.
  10. Equivocal neurological signs and electroencephalo-
       graphic irregularities.

The "sign" approach can serve only as a guideline for the purpose of identification and diagnosis.

The protean nature of the disability is the obvious conclusion from the approach to symptomatology and identification taken above.

The situation, however, is not as irremediable as it might appear. Order is somewhat salvaged by the fact that certain symptoms *do* tend to cluster to form recognizable clinical entities. This is particularly true of the "hyperkinetic syndrome," within the broader context of minimal brain dysfunctioning. The "hypokinetic syndrome," primary reading retardation, and to some extent the aphasias, are other such examples.

Recognition and acceptance of these specific symptom complexes as subcategories, within the general category of minimal brain dysfunctioning, would facilitate classification and the development of appropriate management and education procedures.

DIAGNOSTIC EVALUATION AND CRITERIA

The purposes of the diagnostic evaluation are to demonstrate the existence or absence of minimal brain dysfunction, to determine the causative factors of the past or present environment responsible for this condition, to define the specific limitations of physical or intellectual capabilities present, and thus to establish the basis for a logical program of medical and educational remediation.

Diagnostic confusions have developed from a lack of recognition that differences exist in the objectives of the "medical diagnosis" as opposed to the "educational diagnosis." The objective of the medical diagnosis is to demonstrate the existence of any causative factors of disease or injury capable of amelioration or prevention. The educational diagnosis involves the assessment of performance and capabilities. Its objective is to make possible the establishment of appropriate remedial programs of management and education.

Since the nature and objectives of these two forms of examination are different, the following guidelines for examination include a separate section for each.

GUIDELINES FOR THE DIAGNOSTIC EVALUATION OF DEVIATING CHILDREN

A.   MEDICAL EVALUATION

1. *Histories:*

   a. *Medical*—To include pre-, peri-, and postnatal information. Details of all childhood illnesses should be obtained, including age of child at time of illness, symptoms, severity, course, and care (such as physician in attendance, hospitalization).
   b. *Developmental.*—To include details of motor, language, adaptive, and personal-social development.
   c. *Family-Social.*—To involve parents, child, and others as indicated. The family-social history should include detailed information regarding family constellation, acculturation factors, specific interpersonal family dynamics, emotional stresses, and traumata.

2. *Physical Examination:*

   a. *General.*—To evaluate general physical status and to search for systematic disease. The physical examination should be done as part of the current evaluation of the child, and not obtained at a previous time for some other purpose e.g., routine preschool checkup or in conjunction with a previous illness. Many child study clinics obtain a report on the "physical status" of the child from the family physician or pediatrician as a part of the referral policy. It is not uncommon, however, for the physician simply to fill out the requested form from his records on the child without conducting a current examination.

b. *Neurologic.*—To evaluate neurological function and to search for specific disorders of the nervous system. The developmental aspects of neurologic integration assume primary importance for this examination, especially with reference to integrated motor acts as opposed to simple reflexes.

3. *Special Examinations:*

a. *Ophthalmologic.*—To include visual acuity, fields, and fundi examinations.

b. *Otologic.*—To include audiometric and otoscopic examinations.

4. *Routine Laboratory Tests:*

a. *Serologic.*
b. *Urinalysis.*
c. *Hematologic.*

5. *Special Laboratory Tests (Only When Specifically Indicated):*

a. *Electroencephalographic.*—To include wake, sleep, and serial tracings.
b. *Radiologic.*
c. *Pneumoencephalographic.*
d. *Angiographic.*
e. *Biochemical.*
f. *Genetic assessment: Chromosome analysis.*

B. BEHAVIORAL ASSESSMENT

1. *Academic History:*

a. To involve child's teachers and principal, with their observations regarding school behavior as well as academic progress and achievement. The child's school records, including samples of schoolwork and test results, should be available to the diagnostic team.

2. *Psychological Evaluation:*
The following items represent the core of the psychological evaluation:

a. Individual comprehensive assessment of intellectual functioning.

   b. Measures of complex visual-motor-perceptual functioning.
   c. Behavioral observations in a variety of settings.
   d. Additional indices of learning and behavior as
indicated.

3. *Language Evaluation:*
   Detailed assessment of speech and language behavior.
To include audiometric screening; assessment of articulation, voice quality, and rate; and the expressive and receptive aspects of language.

4. *Educational Evaluation:*
   An educational diagnostician should conduct detailed
analyses of academic abilities, including achievement assessment for details of levels and methods of skill acquisition; e.g., reading, number concepts, spelling and writing.

A child has not had the benefit of a complete diagnostic
evaluation unless he has had both a medical and a behavioral
assessment. The medical evaluation is essential to prevent the
development or continuation of unsuspected disease processes.
The behavioral assessment provides the basis for a logical
management and educational program.

Since various types of diagnosis are involved, a given child
may appropriately receive several diagnoses. Additional confusion stems from the present lack of a multidisciplinary approach. The diagnosis which receives emphasis may reflect a
number of variables including the following:

   1. The diagnostician—his discipline, training, experience,
clinical talents; his knowledge and attitudes regarding causes
in the production of learning and behavior problems in
children.

   2. The diagnostic setting—academic or clinical; community
child guidance center, community all-purpose mental health
clinic, medical center child psychiatry clinic, medical center
pediatric clinic, or private practice. Clinic orientation might
emphasize teaching-training, service, or research.

   3. The diagnostic procedure—including such aspects as

thoroughness and excellence, in terms of time, number, and varieties of techniques and measures utilized and uni- or multiple-disciplinary approach.

Unfortunately, at the present time a lack of scientific knowledge may make it impossible to provide a precise medical or educational diagnosis. Resort must be made to broad and imprecise diagnostic categories. The development of multi-disciplinary diagnostic programs and the continuing increase of scientific knowledge will do much to dispel these existing disturbing uncertainties.

We are dealing with a complex and extensive workup. Few existing clinics are prepared to provide all the services required by this group of children. There are great advantages in consolidation of effort and concentration of facilities in a single environment.

A more detailed consideration of the means by which these needs are to be met and of the specific management and educational programs which will be required is the subject of a further study to be carried out by Task Force II of this mission. The mission of this task force has been defined as follows:

Task Force II will be responsible for consideration of services including those necessary and desirable to diagnose the medical and health-related problem and to identify the methods of determining educational performance capability and ways of educating afflicted children. The two aspects of the problem are education, and medical and health-related services.

1. Relative to the educational aspects of the problem, the task force will concern itself with problems of educational identification, assessment and evaluation, teaching of children with minimal brain dysfunction, educational techniques and methodologies involved, preparation and certification of teachers, responsibility of the public school system for educating these children, guidance of parents in managing children

at home, and public education as it relates to the introduction into society of children with minimal brain dysfunction.

2. Relative to the medical and health-related aspects, the task force will concern itself with methods of identification of children with minimal brain dysfunction, diagnostic services required for obtaining adequate knowledge of the child's ability to perform, and the development of guidelines to be used by appropriate professional persons in conducting and carrying out services necessary to proper management of the child with minimal brain dysfunction.

Appendix B

Comparison of Initial with Subsequent EEG's

A. Patients with 2 EEG records

1. EEG the same in both records

No. of Patients	Type of EEG	Average Age at Initial EEG	Average Age at Subsequent EEG
34	Normal	8.8	11.4
14	6 Hz and 14/6 Hz pos. spikes	9.1	13.1
4	6 Hz pos. spike-waves	7.8	10.0
4	Fast waves	6.9	9.3
1	Slow waves plus other abn.	10	11

2. EEG's both positive but not the same type

No. of Patients	Initial EEG Type	Avg. Age	Subsequent EEG Type	Avg. Age
9	6 Hz and 14/6 Hz pos spikes	9.9	Fast waves	12.2
7	Fast waves	8.6	6 and 14/6 Hz pos. spikes	11.3
2	6 Hz pos. spike-waves	10.5	6 and 14/6 Hz pos. spikes	14.0
2	6 Hz pos. spike-waves	7.0	Fast waves	11.5
1	Fast waves	11	6 Hz pos. spike waves	15
4	Neg. spike-waves	7.0	6 and 14/6 Hz pos. spikes	10.5
2	Neg. spike-waves	7.5	Fast waves	9.5
3	Neg. and diphasic spikes	6.5	6 Hz and 14/6 Hz pos. spikes	11.8
1	Neg. and diphasic spikes	8	Fast waves	13
2	Slow waves plus other abn.	6.0	Fast waves	11.0
1	Slow waves plus other abn.	8	6 and 14/6 Hz pos. spikes	18

3.   Initial EEG normal awake only, subsequent EEG normal awake and asleep, or abnormal.

No. of Patients	Age at Initial EEG	Type of Subsequent EEG	Age at 2nd EEG
10	9.9	Normal awake and asleep	11.0
3	10.0	Fast waves	10.7
4	8.2	6 and 14/6 Hz Pos. spikes	8.4
1	10.0	Slow plus other abnormalities	10.2

4.   Initial EEG normal awake and asleep, subsequent EEG abnormal

No. of Patients	Age at Initial EEG	Type of Subsequent EEG	Age at 2nd EEG
7	8.0	6 and 14/6 Hz pos. spikes	9.6
8	8.4	Fast waves	10.4
4	9.0	Slow plus other abnormalities	11.5

5.   Initial EEG abnormal, subsequent EEG normal

No. of Patients	Age at Initial EEG	Type of Initial EEG	Age at 2nd EEG
5	8.2	6 and 14/6 Hz pos. spikes	11.4
5	8.4	6 Hz pos. spike-waves	12.0
6	7.5	Fast waves	10.3
2	10.0	Neg. and diphasic spikes	13.0
2	10.5	Neg. spike-waves	15.5
1	9	Slow waves	12
3	5.7	Slow waves plus other abnormalities	10.0

B. Patients with more than 2 EEG records

(1)	Age	8	6 Hz pos. spike-waves
		10	Neg. awake only
		13	Neg. awake and asleep
(2)	Age	5	Negative awake and asleep
		9	Fast waves
		14	6 Hz pos. spike-waves
(3)	Age	6	Neg. spikes
		11	Normal awake only
		13	Normal awake and asleep
(4)	Age	11, 15, 17	14/6 Hz pos. spikes
(5)	Age	7	6 Hz pos. spike-waves
		9	Neg. spikes
		12	Neg. spikes
		14	6 Hz pos. spike-waves
(6)	Age	6	6 Hz pos. spike-waves
		8	Normal awake and asleep
		11	Fast waves
(7)	Age	5	Neg. spikes
		7	Fast waves
		10	Fast waves
(8)	Age	7	6 Hz pos. spike-waves
		10	6 Hz pos. spike-waves
		13	Fast waves
(9)	Age	7	Fast waves
		9	14/6 Hz pos. spikes
		12	14/6 Hz pos. spikes
(10)	Age	11	Fast waves
		11¼	14/6 Hz pos. spikes
		14	14/6 Hz pos. spikes

Appendix C

Findings When More Than One Sibling Was Examined

EEG Results—both siblings MBD

	No. of Cases
Both normal	9
Both fast waves	4
Both 14/6 Hz positive spikes	4
Both 6 Hz positive spike-waves	1
One normal, one abnormal	13*
Both abnormal, but different types	19

EEG Results—one sibling MBD, one non-MBD

Both normal	2
MBD sibling abnormal, non-MBD sibling normal	7**

2 sibling-patients in family

1 sibling with MBD, 1 non-MBD	15†
Both MBD	49††
Both non-MBD	8

3 sibling-patients in family

All MBD	11
2 MBD, 1 non-MBD	1

4 sibling-patients in family

All MBD	2
3 MBD, 1 non-MBD	1

* Includes 1 set of adopted, unrelated siblings.
** Includes 1 set of monozygotic twins.
† Includes 2 sets of monozygotic twins.
†† Includes 2 sets of monozygotic twins, 1 set of half-brothers, and 1 set of adopted, unrelated siblings.

Appendix D

EEG Data on Monozygotic Twins
(All Males)

Case Number	Age	Diagnosis of MBD	EEG
Twins A { #438	8	Yes	14/6 Hz positive spikes
Not a case	8	Probably	Normal
Twins B { #442	10	Yes	Normal
#443	10	Yes	Normal
Twins C { #583	7	Yes	Left temporal spikes (same record 7 years later)
Not a case	7	No	Normal
Twins D { #858	10	Yes	14/6 Hz positive spikes
Not a case	10	No	Normal
Twins E { #1011	6	Yes	14/6 Hz positive spikes (normal 23 months later, a few 5-7 Hz slow transients and left temporal 3-5 Hz sharp waves 1 month after the normal record; seizures were present about this time)
#1012	6	Yes	14/6 Hz positive spikes

183

Appendix E

List of Exercises

Used to Develop Coordination,
Body Concept, Spatial Relationships,
Laterality, Dominance and Motor Skills

Cross pattern crawling—forward and backward
Push ups
Pull ups
Sit ups
Bicycle movement on back
Touching floor behind with both feet with a backward roll
Angels in the snow pattern while sighting a fixed point on ceiling
Alternate angels in the snow—sighting a fixed point on ceiling
Dropping back from a kneeling position, touching top of head to
    floor and pulling up with a minimum of hand and arm help
Cross pattern walking—forward and backward
Duck walk
Crab walk—forward and backward
Elephant walk
Seal walk—dragging legs, making arms propel the body
Toe-heel walk
Heel-toe walk
Alternate toe-heel; heel-toe
Skipping
Hopping on dominant foot

Hopping on both feet
Skating movement
Tiptoeing
Balancing on dominant foot while counting—eyes open and then closed
Walking balance beam forward, backward, sideways, while sighting a given target
Cross crawling balance beam (extremely difficult before good coordination is developed)
Walking, hopping, skipping, toe-heeling on stepping stones—forward and backward, eyes open and closed
Going through an obstacle course of increasing difficulty—including soldier crawl, broad jumping, under and over objects, etc.
Eye-tracking a moving object
Eye-tracking with object still and head moving
Counting, beating sticks, etc. to a definite given rhythm
Touching toes
Touching opposite toe—crossing midline
Holding balance while in a squatting position
Jumping rope
Catching, throwing, hitting balls—begin with soft cloth balls
Swinging arms in a circle—forward and backward
Swinging one leg at a time in a circle while balancing on the other
Swinging leg backward, forward, sideways while balancing on the other
Do As I Do—identifying body parts
Do As I Say—identifying body parts
Following directions geared to over, under, in front of, in back of, etc.

Appendix F
Questionnaire in Current Use to Elict Symptoms of Minimal Brain Dysfunction

Child's Name _____ Date of Birth _____

Questionnaire filled out by ☐Mother ☐Father ☐Other (Specify) _____ Date filled out _____

OBSERVATIONS OF BEHAVIOR

For the following traits or problems, please check the box that seems most appropriate.

	No, or rarely	No, used to but not any more	Yes, a little bit	Yes, a fair amount	Yes, very much
Thumb or finger sucking	☐	☐	☐	☐	☐
Restlessness, inability to sit still	☐	☐	☐	☐	☐
Attention-seeking, "show-off" behavior	☐	☐	☐	☐	☐
Skin allergy	☐	☐	☐	☐	☐
Doesn't know how to have fun; behaves like a little adult	☐	☐	☐	☐	☐
Self-consciousness; easily embarrassed	☐	☐	☐	☐	☐
Headaches	☐	☐	☐	☐	☐
Disruptiveness; tendency to annoy and bother others	☐	☐	☐	☐	☐
Feelings of inferiority	☐	☐	☐	☐	☐
Dizziness, vertigo	☐	☐	☐	☐	☐
Boisterousness, rowdiness	☐	☐	☐	☐	☐
Crying over minor annoyances and hurts	☐	☐	☐	☐	☐
Preoccupation; "in a world of his own"	☐	☐	☐	☐	☐
Shyness, bashfulness	☐	☐	☐	☐	☐
Social withdrawal, preference for solitary activities	☐	☐	☐	☐	☐

186

- Dislike for school
- Jealousy over attention paid other children
- Difficulty in bowel control, soiling
- Prefers to play with younger children
- Short attention span
- Lack of self-confidence
- Inattentiveness to what others say
- Easily flustered and confused
- Lack of interest in environment, generally "bored" attitude
- Fighting
- Nausea, vomiting
- Temper tantrums
- Reticence, secretiveness
- Truancy from school
- Hypersensitivity; feelings easily hurt
- Laziness in school and in performance of other tasks
- Anxiety, chronic general fearfulness
- Irresponsibility, undependability
- Excessive daydreaming
- Masturbation
- Hay fever and/or asthma
- Tension, inability to relax
- Disobedience, difficulty in disciplinary control
- Depression, chronic sadness
- Uncooperativeness in group situations
- Aloofness, social reserve
- Passivity, suggestibility; easily led by others
- Clumsiness, awkwardness, poor muscular coordination
- Stuttering
- Hyperactivity; "always on the go"

Columns: Yes, very much | Yes, a fair amount | Yes, a little bit | No, used to but not any more | No, or rarely

Drowsiness _____
Profane language, swearing, cursing _____
Prefers to play with older children _____
Nervousness, jitteriness, jumpiness; easily startled _____
Irritability; hot-tempered, easily aroused to anger _____

Grinds teeth at night _____
Fainting spells _____
Breath-holding spells _____
Head-banging or rocking in bed _____
Sleepwalking _____

Wets self at night (enuresis) _____
Wets self during day _____
Bites nails or fingers _____
Nightmares or night terrors _____
Impulsiveness, acts before thinking _____

Can't "get through" to him or "reach" him _____
Inappropriate lack of fear or cautiousness _____
Stomach aches _____
Specific fears, e.g. of the dark, of dogs, etc. _____
Babyish or unclear speech _____

Lying _____
Stealing _____
Seizures or convulsions or epilepsy _____
Weird or bizarre thoughts or ideas _____
Socially inept or inappropriate behavior _____

Distractibility _____
Destructiveness in regard to his own and/or others' property _____
Negativism, tendency to do the opposite of what is required _____
Impertinence, sauciness, disrespectful _____
Sluggishness, lethargy _____

Danger to self

Danger to others

Excessive talking

Difficulty understanding and following instructions

Upset excessively by new situations

Fire-setting

Cruelty to animals

DURING MEALS

Up and down at table

Interrupts without regard

Wriggling

Fiddles with things

Talks excessively

TELEVISION (if doesn't watch television, check here ☑)

Gets up and down during program

Wriggles

Manipulates objects or body

Talks incessantly

Interrupts

DOING HOMEWORK (if no homework, check here ☐)

Gets up and down

Wriggles

Manipulates objects or body

Talks incessantly

Requires adult supervision or attendance

PLAY

Inability for quiet play

Constantly changing activity

Seeks parental attention

Talks excessively

Disrupts other's play

	No, or rarely	No, used to but not any more	Yes, a little bit	Yes, a fair amount	Yes, very much
SLEEP					
Difficulty settling down for sleep	☐	☐	☐	☐	☐
Inadequate amount of sleep	☐	☐	☐	☐	☐
Restless during sleep	☐		☐	☐	☐
BEHAVIOR AWAY FROM HOME (except Schools)					
Restlessness during travel	☐	☐	☐	☐	☐
Restlessness during shopping (includes touching everything)	☐	☐	☐	☐	☐
Restlessness during church/movies	☐	☐	☐	☐	☐
Restlessness during visiting friends, relatives, etc.	☐	☐	☐	☐	☐
SCHOOL BEHAVIOR (If not in school, check here ☐)					
Up and down	☐	☐	☐	☐	☐
Fidgets, wriggles, touches	☐	☐	☐	☐	☐
Interrupts teacher or other children excessively	☐	☐	☐	☐	☐
Constantly seeks teacher's attention	☐	☐	☐	☐	☐
LEARNING PROBLEMS (if not in school, check here ☐)					
Difficulty with reading	☐	☐	☐	☐	☐
Difficulty with spelling	☐	☐	☐	☐	☐
Difficulty with arithmetic	☐	☐	☐	☐	☐
Difficulty with handwriting	☐	☐	☐	☐	☐

HEALTH HISTORY

Any complications of pregnancy with this child? _____

Any complications of delivery? _____

Birth weight _____ lbs. _____ oz. Condition on birth _____

Any problems with feeding? _____

Age first walked _____ Age first put words together to form sentence _____

Any problems toilet training?
(How long did toilet training take? _____ From _____ To _____)

Age fully toilet trained? _____ Any high fevers - over 105°? _____

Any spells of unconsciousness (describe)? _____

Any serious illnesses? _____

Ever in hospital as bed-patient (other than as newborn)? _____ If "yes" - for what reasons? _____

Right handed ☐ Left handed ☐

REMARKS

Appendix G
Illustrations of EEG Types

Normal Alpha Waves   14/6 Pos. Spikes

6 Hz Pos. Spikes   6 Hz Pos. Spike-Waves

Fast Waves   Negative Spikes

Diphasic Spikes   Neg. Spike-Waves

Notched Waves   Slow Waves

Negative deflections are in upward direction and represent cortical activity; positive deflections are downward and represent activity from deep structures.

Bibliography

Ambrosino, S. V. and Scuto, T. J.: Item analysis: parental attitude vs dextro-amphetamine effect. *Behav. Neuropsychiat.*, 3:19-24, 1971.

Anderson, A. S.: Behavior problems and cerebral dysfunction in children. *Minn. Med.*, 49:305-309, 1966.

Anderson, W. W.: Hyperkinetic child: neurological appraisal. *Neurology*, 13: 968, 1963.

Andy, O. J. and Jurko, M. F.: Focal thalamic discharges with visceral disturbance and pain treated by thalamotomy. *Clin. Electroenceph.*, 3:215-223, 1972.

Anthony, E. J.: A psychodynamic model of minimal brain dysfunction. *Ann. N.Y. Acad. Sci.*, 205:52-60, 1973.

Arnold, L. E. et. al.: Hyperkinetic adult: study of the paradoxical amphetamine response. *J.A.M.A.*, 222:693-694, 1972.

Arnold, L. E.: The art of medicating hyperkinetic children. A number of practical suggestions. *Clin. Pediatr.* (Phila.), 12:35-41, 1973.

Arnold, L. E. et. al.: Levoamphetamine and dextroamphetamine: comparative efficacy in the hyperkinetic syndrome. Assessment by target symptoms. *Arch. Gen. Psychiat.*, 27:816-822, 1972.

Arnold, L. E. et. al.: Levoamphetamine and dextroamphetamine: differential effect on aggression and hyperkinesis in children and dogs. *Am. J. Psychiat.*, 130:165-170, 1973.

Bailey, P.: The great psychiatric revolution. *Am. J. Psychiat.*, 113:387-406, 1956.

Bailey, P.: Modern attitudes toward the relationship of the brain to behavior. *Arch. Gen. Psychiat.*, 2:361-378, 1960.

Bakwin, H.: Benzedrine in behavior disorders of children. *J. Pediat.*, 32-215, 1948.

BARCAI, A.: The emergence of neurotic conflict in some children after successful administration of dextroamphetamine. *J. Child Psychol. Psychiat.*, 10: 269-276, 1969.

BARCAI, A.: Predicting the response of children with learning disabilities and behavior problems to dextroamphetamine sulfate. The clinical interview and the finger twitch test. *Pediatrics*, 47:79-80, 1971.

BARNARD, K. AND COLLAR, B. S.: Minimal brain dysfunction. V. Diagnosis and treatment. C. Non-drug treatment. Early diagnosis, interpretation, and intervention: a commentary on the nurse's role. *Ann. N. Y. Acad. Sci.*, 205:373-382, 1973.

BATEMAN, B. D.: Educational implications of minimal brain dysfunction. *Ann. N. Y. Acad. Sci.*, 205:245-250, 1973.

BATTLE, E. S., LACEY, B.: A context for hyperactivity in children, over time. *Child Dev.*, 43:757-773, 1972

BAX, M.: The active and the over-active school child. *Dev. Med. Child Neurol.*, 14:83-86, 1972.

BAYRAKAL, S.: The significance of electroencephalographic abnormality in behavior-problem children. *Can. Psychiat. Assoc. J.*, 10:387-391, 1965.

BAZELL, R. J.: Panel sanctions amphetamines for hyperkinetic children. *Science*, 171:1223, 1971.

BELL, R. Q. ET AL.: A rating system for the assessment of hyperactive and withdrawn children in preschool samples. *Am. J. Orthopsychiat.*, 42:23-34, 1972.

BENDER, L.: Organic brain conditions producing behavior disturbances, in Lewis, N.D.C., Pacella, R. C. (Eds.). *Recent Trends in Child Psychiatry*. New York, International Universities Press, 1946.

BENDER, L.: *Psychopathology of Children with Organic Brain Disorders.*, Springfield, Ill., Charles C Thomas, 1959.

BENDER, L.: The brain and child behavior. *Arch. Gen. Psychiat.*, 4:531-547, 1961.

BENTON, A. L.: Minimal brain dysfunction from a neuropsychological point of view. *Ann. N. Y. Acad. Sci.*, 205:29-37, 1973.

BIRCH, H. G. (Ed.): *Brain Damage in Children—The Biological and Social Aspects*. Baltimore, Williams & Wilkins, 1964.

BOELHOUWER, C. ET. AL.: Positive spiking: double-blind control study on its significance in behavior disorders, both diagnostically and therapeutically. *Am. J. Psychiat.*, 125: 473-481, 1968.

BRADLEY, C.: The behavior of children receiving Benzedrine. *Am. J. Psychiat.*, 94:577-585, 1937.

BRANDON, S.: Overactivity in childhood. *J. Psychosom. Res.*, 15:411-415, 1971.

BROWN, D. ET. AL.: Imipramine therapy and seizures: three children treated for hyperactive behavior disorders. *Am. J. Psychiat.*, 130:210-212, 1973.

BRUMLIK, J. AND MORETTI, L.: The effect of diphenylhydantoin on nerve conduction velocity. *Neurology*, 16:1217-1218, 1966.

CAMP, B. W.: WISC perfromance in acting-out and delinquent children with and without EEG abnormality. *J. Cons. Psychol.*, 30:350-353, 1966.

CAMPBELL, M. ET. AL.: Lithium and chlorpromazine: a controlled crossover study of hyperactive severely disturbed young children. *J. Autism Child. Schizo.*, 2:234-263, 1972.

CANTWELL, D. P.: Psychiatric illness in families of hyperactive children. *Arch. Gen. Psychiat.* 27:414-417, 1972.

CHEN, C. C. AND HIGGINS, C.: Children's behavior disorders and EEG patterns. *Dis. Nerv. Syst.* 27:52-56, 1966.

CHESS, S.: Diagnosis and treatment of the hyperactive child. *N. Y. J. Med.,* 60:2379-2385, 1959.

CLAGHORN, J. ET AL.: The effect of drugs on hyperactivity in children with some observations of changes in mineral metabolism. *J. Nerv. Ment. Dis.,* 153: 118-125, 1971.

CLEMENTS, S. D. AND PETERS, J. E.: Minimal brain dysfunctions in school-age child. *Arch. Gen. Psychiat.* 6:185-197, 1962.

CLEMENTS, S. D.: *Minimal Brain Dysfunction in Children.* U.S. Dept. of Health, Education and Welfare, Public Health Service Publication No. 1415, 1966.

CLEMENTS, S. D.: The child with minimal brain dysfunction: a multidisciplinary catalyst. *J. Lancet* 86:121-123, 1966.

CLEMENTS, S. D. AND PETERS, J. E.: Psychoeducational programming for children with minimal brain dysfunctions. *Ann. N. Y. Acad. Sci.,* 205:46-51, 1973.

CLEMMENS, R. L. AND KENNY, T. J.: Clinical correlates of learning disabilities, minimal brain dysfunction and hyperactivity. *Clin. Pediatr.* (Phila.), 11: 311-313, 1972.

COHEN, N. J. ET. AL.: Cognitive styles in adolescents previously diagnosed as hyperactive. *J. Child Psychol. Psychiat.,* 13:203-209, 1972.

COHEN, N. J. ET. AL.: The effect of methylphenidate on attentive behavior and autonomic activity in hyperactive children. *Psychopharmacologia,* 22: 282-294, 1971.

COHEN, S. A.: Minimal brain dysfunction and practical matters such as teaching kids to read. *Ann. N. Y. Acad. Sci.,* 205:251-261, 1973.

COHN, R.: Delayed acquisition of reading and writing abilities in children: a neurological study. *Arch. Neurol.* 4: 153-164, 1961.

COLEMAN, M.: Serotonin concentrations in whole blood of hyperactive children. *J. Pediat.,* 78:985-990, 1971.

CONNERS, C. K.: The syndrome of minimal brain dysfunction: psychological aspects. *Ped. Clin. N. Amer.* 14: 749-766, 1967.

CONNERS, C. K. ET AL.: Effect of dextroamphetamine on children. *Arch. Gen. Psychiat.* 17:478-485, 1967.

CONNERS, C. K. ET AL.: Magnesium pemoline and dextroamphetamine: a controlled study in children with minimal brain dysfunction. *Psychopharmacologia,* 26:321-336, 1972.

CONNERS, C. K.: Psychological assessment of children with minimal brain dysfunction. *Ann. N. Y. Acad. Sci.,* 205:283-302, 1973.

CORSON, S. A. ET AL.: Tranquilizing effect of d-amphetamine on hyperkinetic untrainable dogs. *Fed. Proc.* 30:106, 1971.

CUTTS, K. K. AND JASPER, H. H.: Effect of Benzedrine sulfate and phenobarbital on behavior problem children with abnormal electroencephalograms. *Arch. Neurol. Psychiat.,* 41:1138, 1939.

DAVEAU, M.: EEG of 150 children with behavior disorders. *Electroenceph. Clin. Neurophysiol.,* 10:198, 1958.

DAVID, O. ET AL.: Lead and hyperactivity. *Lancet* 2:900-903, 1972.

DE HIRSCH, K.: Early language development and minimal brain dysfunction. *Ann. N. Y. Acad. Sci.*, 205:158-163, 1973.

DELONG, A. R.: What have we learned from psychoactive drug research on hyperactives. *Am. J. Dis. Child.*, 123:177-180, 1972.

DEMERDASH, A. ET AL.: The incidence of 14 and 6 per second positive spikes in a population of normal children. *Develop. Med. Child Neurol.*, 10: 309-316, 1968.

DENHOFF, E.: The natural life history of children with minimal brain dysfunction. *Ann. N. Y. Acad. Sci.*, 205:188-205, 1973.

DIMITROFF, M. L.: Motor skills of hypereractive children. *Am. J. Orthopsychiat.* 42:746, 1972.

DYKMAN, R. A. ET AL.: Experimental approaches to the study of minimal brain dysfunction: a follow-up study. *Ann. N. Y. Acad. Sci.*, 205:93-108, 1973.

EISENBERG, L.: The management of the hyperkinetic child. *Develop. Med. Child Neurol.*, 8:593-598, 1966.

EISENBERG, L.: Symposium on behavior modification by drugs. 3. The clinical use of stimulant drugs in children. *Pediatrics*, 49:709-715, 1972.

EISENBERG, L.: The hyperkinetic child and stimulant drugs. *New Eng. J. Med.*, 287:249-250, 1972.

ELLINGSON, R. J.: Incidence of EEG abnormality among patients with mental disorder of apparently non-organic origin: critical review. *Am. J. Psychiat.*, 111:263. 1954.

EPSTEIN, L. C. ET AL.: Correlation of dextroamphetamine excretion and drug response in hyperkinetic children. *J. Nerv. Ment. Dis.*, 146:136-146, 1968.

ERENBERG, G.: Mood-altering drugs and hyperkinetic children. *Pediatrics*, 49: 308-311, 1972.

FISCHER, K. C. AND WILSON, W. P.: Methylphenidate and the hyperkinetic state. *Dis. Nerv. Syst.*, 32:695-698, 1971.

FISH, B.: The "one child, one drug" myth of stimulants in hyperkinesis. *Arch. Gen. Psychiat.* 25:193-203, 1971.

FISH, B.: Treating hyperactive children. *J.A.M.A.*, 218:1427, 1971.

FREEMAN, R. D.: The drug treatment of learning disorders: continuing confusion. *J. Pediatr.*, 81:112-115, 1972.

GALLAGHER, J. J.: New educational treatment models for children with minimal brain dysfunction. *Ann. N. Y. Acad. Sci.*, 205:383-389, 1973.

GALLAGHER, J. R. ET AL.: Relation between the electrical activity of the cortex and the personality in adolescent boys. *Psychosom. Med.*, 4:134-139, 1942.

GARDNER, L. I. AND NEU, R. L.: Evidence linking an extra Y chromosome to sociopathic behavior. *Arch. Gen. Psychiat.*, 26:220-222, 1972.

GAZZANIGA, M. S.: The split brain in man. *Scientific American*, 217:24-29, 1967.

GAZZANIGA, M. S.: Brain theory and minimal brain dysfunction. *Ann. N. Y. Acad.Sci.*, 205:89-92, 1973.

GIANTURCO, D. ET AL.: Effect of psychiatric and autonomic symptoms on the incidence of fourteen-and-six per second positive spikes among adolescents. *Clin. Electroenceph.*, 3:55-59, 1972.

GIBBS, E. L. AND GIBBS, F. A.: Electroencephalographic evidence of thalamic and hypothalamic epilepsy. *Neurology*, 1:136, 1951.

GIBBS, F. A. AND GIBBS, E. L.: Fourteen and six per second positive spikes. *Electroenceph. Clin. Neurophys.*, 15:553-558, 1963.

GIBBS, F. A. AND GIBBS, E. L.: Borderland of epilepsy. *J. Neuropsychiat.*, 4: 287-295, 1963.

GIBBS, F. A. AND GIBBS, E. L.: *Atlas of Electroencephalography* Vol. 3. Cambridge, Mass., Addison-Wesley, 1964.

GLASER, G. H.: *EEG and Behavior.* New York, Basic Books, 1963.

GOMEZ, M. R.: Minimal cerebral dysfunction (maximal neurologic confusion). *Clin. Pediat.*, 6:589-591, 1967.

GREEN, J. B.: Association of behavior disorder with electroencephalographic focus in children without seizures. *Neurology*, 11:337, 1961.

GREENBERG, L. M. ET AL.: Effects of dextroamphetamine, chlorpromazine, and hydroxyzine on behavior and performance in hyperactive children. *Am. J. Psychiat.*, 129:532-539, 1972.

GROSS, M. D., WILSON, W. C.: Behavior disorders of children with cerebral dysrhythmias. *Arch. Gen. Psychiat.*, 11:610-619, 1964.

GROSS, M. D.: Violence associated with organic brain disease, in Fawcett, J. (Ed). *Dynamics of Violence*, Chicago, American Medical Assn., 1971.

HANSON, L.: Biochemical and behavioral effects of tyrosine hydroxylase inhibition. *Psychopharmacologia*, 11:8-17, 1967.

HANVIK, L. J. ET AL.: Diagnosis of cerebral dysfunction in child. *Am. J. Dis. Child*, 101:364-375, 1961.

HARLIN, V. K.: Help for the hyperkinetic child in school. *J. Sch. Health*, 42: 587-92, 1972.

HENRY, C. E.: Positive spike discharges in EEG and behavior abnormality, in Glaser, G. H., (Ed.): *EEG and Behavior*, New York, Basic Books, 1963.

HERTZIG, M. E. AND BIRCH, H.: Neurologic organization in psychiatrically disturbed abolescents. *Arch. Gen. Psychiat.*, 19:528-537, 1968.

HEWETT, F. M.: Conceptual models for viewing minimal brain dysfunction developmental psychology and behavioral modification. *Ann. N. Y. Acad. Sci.*, 205:38-45, 1973.

HOFFER, A.: Treatment of hyperkinetic children with nicotinamide and pyridoxine. *Can. Med. Assoc. J.*, 107:111-112, 1972.

HOWELL, M. C. ET AL.: Hyperactivity in children: types, diagnosis, drug therapy, approaches to management. *Clin. Pediatr.* (Phila.), 11:30-39, 1972.

HUGHES, J. ET AL.: Electroclinical correlations in the positive spike phenomenon. *Electroenceph. Clin. Neurophys.*, 13:599-605, 1961.

HUGHES, J. ET AL.: Electro-clinical correlations in the six-per-second spike and wave complex. *Electroenceph. Clin. Neurophys.*, 18:71-77, 1965.

HUGHES, J.: A review of the positive spike phenomenon, in Wilson, W. (Ed): *Applications of Electroencephalography in Psychiatry.* Durham, N. C., Duke University Press, 1965.

HUSBAND, P. AND HINTON, P. E.: Families of children with repeated accidents. *Arch. Dis. Childhood*, 47:396-400, 1972.

JASPER, H. H. ET AL.: EEG analyses of behavior problem children. *Am. J. Psychiat.* 95:641, 1938.

JONES, E. ET AL.: Focal abnormalities of the electroencephalogram in juveniles with behavior disorders. *J. Nerv. Ment. Dis.*, 122:28, 1955.

KAHN, E., COHEN, L. H.: Organic drivenness—a brain stem syndrome and an experience—with case reports. *New. Eng. J. Med.*, 210:748-756, 1934.

KALVERBOER, A. F. ET AL.: Follow-up of infants at risk of minor brain dysfunction. *Ann. N. Y. Acad. Sci.*, 205:173-187, 1973.

KALYANARAMAN, K. ET AL.: Maple syrup urine disease (branched-chain ketoaciduria) variant type manifesting as hyperkinetic behavior and mental retardation. Report of two cases. *J. Neurol. Sci.*, 15:209-217, 1972.

KANNER, L.: Early infantile autism. *Am. J. Orthopsychiat.*, 19:416-426, 1949.

KELLAWAY, A. M. ET AL.: A specific electroencephalographic correlate of convulsive equivalent disorders in children. *J. Pediat.*, 55:582-592, 1959.

KENNARD, M. A.: Inheritance of electroencephalographic patterns in the families of children with behavior disorders. *Tr. Am. Neurol. A.*, 72:177-179, 1947.

KENNY, T. J. ET AL.: Characteristics of children referred because of hyperactivity. *J. Pediatr.*, 79:618-622, 1971.

KETY, S. S. ET AL.: Mental illness in the biological and adoptive families of adopted schizophrenics. *Am. J. Psychiat.*, 128:302-306, 1971.

KINSBOURNE, M.: Minimal brain dysfunction as a neurodevelopmental lag. *Ann. N. Y. Acad. Sci.*, 205:268-273, 1973.

KLINKERFUSS, G. H. ET AL.: Electroencephalographic abnormalities of children with hyperkinetic behavior. *Neurology*, 15:883-891, 1965.

KNIGHTS, R. M.: Problems of criteria in diagnosis: a profile similarity approach. *Ann. N. Y. Acad. Sci.*, 205:124-131, 1973.

KNOBEL, M. ET AL.: Hyperkinesis and organicity in children. *Arch. Gen. Psychiat.*, 1:310-321, 1959.

KNOBEL, M.: Psychopharmacology for the hyperkinetic child. *Arch. Gen. Psychiat.*, 6:198-202, 1962.

KNOBLOCH, H. AND PASAMANICK, B.: Syndrome of minimal cerebral damage in infancy. *J.A.M.A.*, 170:1384-1387, 1959.

KRAKOWSKI, A. J.: Amitriptyline in treatment of hyperkinetic children. *Psychosomatic Med.* 6:355-360, 1965.

KRAMER, F., POLLNOW, H.: Ueber eine hyperkinetische erkrankung im kindesalter. *Monatschr. Psychiat. Neurol.*, 82:1-40, 1932.

KURLAND, A.: Placebo effect, in Uhr, L., Miller, J. (Eds.): *Drugs and Behavior.* New York, Wiley, 1960.

LANDSVREUGD, C., BEECKMANS-BALLE, M.: Study of WISC verbal and performance quotients in population of children with educational problems. *Rev. Neuropsychiat. Infant.*, 16:219-226, 1968.

LAUFER, M. W., DENHOFF, E.: Hyperkinetic syndrome in children. *J. Pediat.*, 50:463, 1957.

LAUFER, M. W.: Psychiatric diagnosis and treatment of children with minimal brain dysfunction. *Ann. N. Y. Acad. Sci.*, 205:303-309, 1973.

LESSER, L. L.: Hyperkinesis in children. Operational approach to management. *Clin. Pediat.* (Phila.), 9:548-552, 1970.

LITTLE, S. C.: General analysis of the correlates of the "fourteen and six" per second dysrhythmia. Read at the Sixth International Congress of EEG and Clinical Neurophysiology, Vienna, September 7, 1965.

LOMBROSO, C. T. ET AL.: Ctenoids in healthy youths. Controlled study of 14 and 6-per-second positive spiking. *Neurology*, 16:1152, 1966.

McCARTHY, J. M.: Minimal brain dysfunction. V. Diagnosis and treatment.

C. Non-drug treatment. Education: the base of the triangle. *Ann. N. Y, Acad. Sci.,* 205:362-367, 1973.

McNamara, J. J.: Hyperactivity in the apartment-bound child. *Clin. Pediatr.* (Phila.), 11:371-372, 1972.

Mehegan, C. C., Dreifus, F. E.: A neurological study of reading disability. *Virginia Med. Monthly,* 94:453-459, 1967.

Mendelson, W. et al.: Hyperactive children as teenagers: a follow-up study. *J. Nerv. Ment. Dis.,* 153:273-279, 1971.

Menkes, M. M. et al.: A twenty-five year follow-up study on the hyperkinetic child with minimal brain dysfunction. *Pediatrics,* 39:393-399, 1967.

Michaels, J. J. and Secunda, L.: The relationship of neurotic traits to EEG in children with behavior disorder. *Am. J. Psychiat.,* 101:407, 1944.

Millichap, J. G. and Fowler, G. W.: Treatment of "Minimal Brain Dysfunction" syndrome. *Ped. Clin. North Amer.,* 14:767-777, 1967.

Millichap, J. G. et al.: Hyperkinetic behavior and learning disorders. *Am. J. Dis. Child.,* 116:235-244, 1968.

Millichap, J. G.: Drugs in management of hyperkinetic and perceptually handicapped children. *J.A.M.A.,* 206:1527-1530, 1968.

Millichap, J. G.: Drugs in management of minimal brain dysfunction. *Ann. N. Y. Acad. Sci.,* 205:321-334, 1973.

Milman, D.: Organic behavior disorder. *J. Dis. Child,* 91:521-528, 1956.

Milstein, V. and Small, J.: Psychological correlates of fourteen and six positive spikes, six-per-second spike and wave, and small spike sharp transients. *Clin. Electroenceph.,* 2:206-212, 1971.

Minskoff, J. G.: Minimal brain dysfunction. 3. Epidemiology. Differential approaches to prevalence estimates of learning disabilities. *Ann. N. Y. Acad. Sci.,* 205:139-145, 1973.

Mofenson, H. C. et al.: Detection of the hyperactive child. *J. Pediatr.,* 80: 687, 1972.

Morris, D. P. and Dozier, E.: Childhood behavior disorders: subtler organic factors. *Texas State J. Med.,* 57:134-138, 1961.

Morrison, J. R., Stewart, M. A.: A family study of the hyperactive child syndrome. *Biol. Psychiat.* 3: 189-197, 1971.

Ney, P. G.: Psychosis in a child, associated with amphetamine administration. *Can. Med. Assoc. J.,* 97:1026-1029, 1967.

Nichamin, S. J., Barahal G. D.: Faulty neurologic integration with perceptual disorders in children. *Mich. Med.,* 67:1071-1075, 1968.

Ounsted, C.: Hyperkinetic syndrome in epileptic children. *Lancet,* 2:303, 1955.

Paine, R. S.: Minimal chronic brain syndromes in children. *Dev. Med. Child Neurol.,* 4:21-27, 1962.

Paine, R. S. et al.: A study of minimal cerebral dysfunction. *Develop. Med. Child Neurol.,* 10:505-520, 1968.

Palkes, H. and Stewart, M.: Intellectual ability and performance of hyperactive children. *Am. J. Orthopsychiat.,* 42:35-9, 1972.

Pasamanick, B.: Anticonvulsant drug therapy of behavior problem children with abnormal electroencephalograms. *Arch. Neurol. Psychiat.,* 65:752, 1951.

Perel, J. M. et al.: Inhibition of imipramine metabolism by methylphenidate. *Fed. Proc.,* 28:418, 1969.

Perlstein, M. A.: The use of a monoamine oxidase inhibitor (Catron) in behavior disturbances in children, in Featherstone, R., Simon, A. (Eds.): *Pharmacological Study of the Mind.* Springfield, Ill., Charles C Thomas, 1959.

PETERSEN, I. AND AKESSON, H. O.: EEG studies of siblings of children showing 14 and 6 per second positive spikes. *Acta. Genet.*, 18:163-169, 1968.

PETERSEN, I. ET AL.: Paroxysmal activity in EEG of normal children, in Kellaway, P. and Petersen, I. (Eds.): *Clinical Electroencephalography of Children.* Stockholm, Almqvist and Wiksell, 1968, pp. 167-187.

PETERSON, D. R.: Behavior problems of middle childhood. *J. Consult. Psychol.*, 25:205-209, 1961.

PINCUS, J. H., GLASER, G. H.: The syndrome of minimal brain damage in childhood. *New Eng. J. Med.*, 275:27-35, 1966.

POND, D. A.: EEG in Paediatrics, in Hill, D., Parr, G. (Eds): *Electroencephalography.* New York, The Macmillan Co., 1963.

QUAY, H. C.: Personality dimensions in delinquent males as inferred from the factor analysis of behavior ratings. *J. Res. Crime Delinquency*, 1:33-37, 1964.

RANDRUP, A. AND MUNKVAD, I.: Pharmacological studies on the brain mechanisms underlying two forms of behavioral excitation: stereotyped hyperactivity and "rage." *Ann. N. Y. Acad. Sci.*, 159:928-938, 1969.

RAPOPORT, J.: Childhood behavior and learning problems treated with imipramine. *Int. J. Neuropsychiat.*, 1:635-642, 1965.

RAPOPORT, J. L. ET AL.: Urinary noradrenaline and playroom behavior in hyperactive boys. *Lancet* 2:1141, 1970.

REITAN, R. M., BOLL, T. J.: Neuropsychological correlates of minimal brain dysfunction. *Ann. N. Y. Acad. Sci.*, 205:65-88, 1973.

RIMLAND, B.: *Infantile Autism—The Syndrome and its Implications for a Neural Theory of Behavior.* New York, Appleton-Century-Crofts, 1964.

RODIN, E. A.: Familial occurrence of the 14 and 6/sec positive spike phenomenon. *Electroenceph. Clin. Neurophys.*, 17:566-570, 1964.

ROSENBLOOM, L.: Learning disabilities and hyperkinesis. *Dev. Med. Child Neurol.*, 14:394-395, 1972.

ROSENTHAL, D. AND KETY, S. S. (Eds.): *The Transmission of Schizophrenia.* New York, Pergamon Press, 1968.

ROSENTHAL, D. ET AL.: The adopted-away offspring of schizophrenics. *Am. J. Psychiat.*, 128:307-311, 1971.

SAFER, D. J.: Drugs for problem school children. *J. Sch. Health*, 41:491-495, 1971.

SAFER, D. J. AND ALLEN, R. P.: Factors influencing the suppressant effects of two stimulant drugs on the growth of hyperactive children. *Pediat.*, 51: 660-667, 1973.

SAFER, D. ET AL.: Depression of growth in hyperactive children on stimulant drugs. *New Eng. J. Med.*, 287:217-220, 1972.

SATTERFIELD, J. H. ET AL.: Physiological studies of the hyperkinetic child. *Am. J. Psychiat.*, 128:1418-1424, 1972.

SATTERFIELD, J. H. ET AL.: EEG aspects in the diagnosis and treatment of minimal brain dysfunction. *Ann. N. Y. Acad. Sci.*, 205:274-282, 1973.

SAUNDERS, J. C.: Phenelzine in childhood and adolescent psychiatric disturbances. Paper presented before section in Child Psychiatry, Pan American Medical Congress, 1960.

SCANLON, J.: Treatment of hyperkinetic child with dextroamphetamine and ephedrine. *Pediatrics*, 46:975-976, 1970.

SCHAIN, R. J.: Neurological evaluation of children with learning disorders. *Neuropaediatrie*, 1:307-317, 1970.

SCHECKEL, C. L. ET AL.: Hyperactive states related to the metabolism of norepinephrine and smiliar biochemicals. *Ann. N. Y. Acad. Sc.*, 159:939-958, 1969.

SCHILDKRAUT, J. ET AL.: Norepinephrine metabolism and drug used in the affective disorders: a possible mechanism of action. *Am. J. Psychiat.*, 124: 600-608, 1967.

SCHRAGER, J., LINDY, J.: Hyperkinetic children: early indicators of potential school failure. *Community Ment. Health. J.* 6:447-454, 1970.

SCHWALB, E.: Clinical considerations of cerebral dysfunction in children. *N. Y. State J. Med.*, 76:2320-2324, 1967.

SCHWARTZ, L.: The use and misuse of parental guilt in cases of children with minimal brain dysfunction. *Ann. N. Y. Acad. Sci.*, 205:368-372, 1973.

SEASHORE, H. G, ET AL.: The standardization of the Wechsler Intelligence Scale for Children. *J. Consult. Psychol.*, 14:99-110, 1950.

SEASHORE, H. G.: Differences between verbal and performance IQ's on the Wechsler Intelligence Scale for Children. *J. Consult. Psychol.*, 15:62-67, 1951,

SECUNDA, L. AND FINLEY, K. H.: Electroencephalographic disorders in children presenting behavior disorders. *New Eng. J. Med.*, 226:850, 1942.

SHETTY, T.: Photic responses in hyperkinesis of childhood. *Science*, 174:1356-1357, 1971.

SHETTY, T.: Alpha rhythms in the hyperkinetic child. *Nature* (Lond), 234: 476, 1971.

SMALL, A. ET AL.: Effects of dextroamphetamine sulfate on EEG sleep patterns of hyperactive children. *Arch. Gen. Psychiat.*, 25:369-380, 1971.

SMALL, J.: The six-per-second spike and wave—a psychiatric population study. *Electroenceph. Clin. Neurophys.*, 24:561-568, 1968.

SMITH, B. S. AND PHILLIPS, E. H.: Treating a hyperactive child. *Phys. Ther.*, 50:506-510, 1970.

SNYDER, S. H., MEYERHOFF, J. L.: How amphetamine acts in minimal brain dysfunction. *Ann. N. Y. Acad. Sci.*, 205:310-320, 1973.

SOLOMONS, G.: Minimal brain dysfunction. V. Diagnosis and treatment. B. Drug treatment. Drug therapy: initiation and follow-up. *Ann. N. Y. Acad. Sci.*, 205:335-344, 1973.

SPRAGUE, R. L.: Minimal brain dysfunction from a behavioral viewpoint. *Ann. N. Y. Acad. Sci.*, 205:349-361, 1973.

STEVENS, A., WEHRHEIM, H. K.: Psychiatry and juvenile delinquency. *Behavioral Neuropsychiat.*, 1:14-20, 1969.

STEWART, M. A.: As reported in the *Chicago Tribune*, April 1973.

STRAUSS, A. A. AND LEHTINEN, L.: *Psychopathology and Education of the Brain Injured Child*. New York: Grune & Stratton, 1947.

STRAUSS, A. A. AND KEPHART, N.: *Psychopathology and Education of the Brain Injured Child Vol. II*. New York: Grune & Stratton, 1955.

STROTHER, C. R.: Minimal Cerebral Dysfunction: a historical overview. *Ann. N. Y. Acad. Sci.*, 205:6-17, 1973.

SYKES, D. H. ET AL.: The effect of methylphenidate (Ritalin) on sustained attention in hyperactive children. *Psychopharmacologia,* 25:262-274, 1972.

SYKES, D. H. ET AL.: Attention in hyperactive children and the effort of methylphenidate (Ritalin). *J. Child Psychol. Psychiat.,* 12:129-39, 1971.

TEC, L., LEVY, H. B.: Amphetamines in hyperkinetic children. *J.A.M.A.,* 216: 1864-1865, 1971.

TEC, L.: Hyperkinetic children and the staccato syndrome. *Am. J. Psychiat.,* 130:330, 1973.

THOMAS, A. ET AL.: *Behavioral Individuality in Early Childhood.* New York: New York University Press, 1963.

THOMAS, A. ET AL.: *Temperament and Behavior Disorders in Children.* New York: New York University Press, 1968.

TRIANTAFILLOU, M.: Pemoline in overactive mentally handicapped children. *Br. J. Psychiat.,* 121:577, 1972.

TURNER, W. J., MERLIS, S.: Clinical correlations between electroencephalography and antisocial behavior. *Med. Times,* 90:505, 1962.

VANDENBERG, S. G.: Possible hereditary factors in minimal brain dysfunction. *Ann. N. Y. Acad. Sci.,* 205:223-230, 1973.

WALDROP, M. F. AND GOERING, J. D.: Hyperactivity and minor physical anomalies in elementary school children. *Am. J. Orthopsychiat.,* 41:602-607, 1971.

WALKER, C. F. AND KIRKPATRICK, B. B.: Dilantin treatment for behavior problem children with abnormal electroencephalograms. *Am. J. Psychiat.,* 103: 484, 1947.

WALTER, R. D. ET AL.: A controlled study of the fourteen-and-six-per-second EEG pattern. *Arch. Gen. Psychiat.,* 2:559, 1960.

WEISS, G. ET AL.: Studies on the hyperactive child. *Arch. Gen. Psychiat.,* 24: 409-414, 1971.

WEISS, G. ET AL.: Comparison of the effects of chlorpromazine, dextroamphetamine and methylphenidate on the behavior and intellectual functioning of hyperactive children. *Can. Med. Assoc. J.,* 104:20-25, 1971.

WENDER, P. H.: The role of genetics in the etiology of the schizophrenias. *Am. J. Orthopsychiat.,* 39:447-458, 1969.

WENDER, P. H.: *Minimal Brain Dysfunction in Children.* New York, Wiley & Son, 1971.

WENDER, P. H.: Some speculations concerning a possible biochemical basis of minimal brain dysfunction. *Ann. N. Y. Acad. Sci.,* 205:18-28, 1973.

WERRY, J. S.: Studies on the hyperactive child: an empirical analysis of the minimal brain dysfunction syndrome. *Arch. Gen. Psychiat.,* 19:9-16, 1968.

WERRY, J. S. ET AL.: Studies on the hyperactive child: neurologic status compared with neurotic and normal children. *Am. J. Orthopsychiat.,* 42:441-451, 1972.

WHITEHEAD, P. L., CLARK, L. D.: Effect of lithium carbonate, placebo, and thioridazine on hyperactive children. *Am. J. Psychiat.,* 127:824-825, 1970.

WILLERMAN, L.: Social aspects of minimal brain dysfunction. *Ann. N. Y. Acad. Sci.,* 205:164-172, 1973.

WILSON, W. P., HARRIS, B. S. H.: Psychiatric problems in children with frontal, central and temporal lobe epilepsy. *South. Med. J.,* 59:49-53, 1966.

Index

absorption, problem with medication, 77-79
acetazolamide, 65, 134, 135
accident proneness, 55, 123
addiction, 108, 150
adolescence, 47, 81, 82, 99, 103, 107, 111, 138, 139, 145, 151
adverse reactions, 19, 85, 95-98, 145
age, 14, 23-25, 34, 41, 46, 48, 138
aggressiveness, 4, 26-28
Akesson, H. O., 138
Allen, R. P., 98
aminoaciduria, 49, 78
amitriptyline, 65, 81, 136
amphetamines, 4, *see also* d-amphetamine, r-amphetamine
Andy, O. J., 140
anorexia, 97, 98, 106, 107, 145, 152
anti-convulsants, 65, 66, 81, 137, 138, 144, 148
aphasia, 17, 37, 50, 60, 75, 134, 135
apraxia, 37
attention span, 4, 5, 19, 20, 31, 32, 52, 53, 130, 146
autism, 3, 27, 50, 51, 75, 127

behavior
  problems of, 26-32, 39, 50, 53-55, 57-60, 111, 113, 115-120, 127-129

improvement in, 57, 62, 63, 68-85, 111, 113, 115-117, 120, 127-129, 144, 145
Bender-Gestalt test, 20, 85, 129, 148
Bender, L., 3
Benzedrine, *see* r-amphetamine
Birch, H. G., 4
blood pressure, 107
Bradley, C., 4
brain, 2, 3
  damage, 1, 4, 5, 17, 21, 44, 45, 50, 51, 73, 75, 82, 138, 145, 149
Brumlik, J., 138

Cantwell, D. P., 138
carbon monoxide poisoning, 50
catecholamines, 64-66
Celontin, 65, *see also* methsuximide
Chess, S., 4
chief complaints, 25-28, 31, 32
chlorpromazine, 65
Clements, S. D., 5
Cohen, L. H., 4
Coleman, M., 137
colic, 52, 110
controls, 11, 22, 23, 29-31, 37, 38, 71, 72, 140
control systems, 28, 32, 55, 84, 137, 149

203